MENSA
GUIDE TO
chess

30 days to great chess
Burt Hochberg

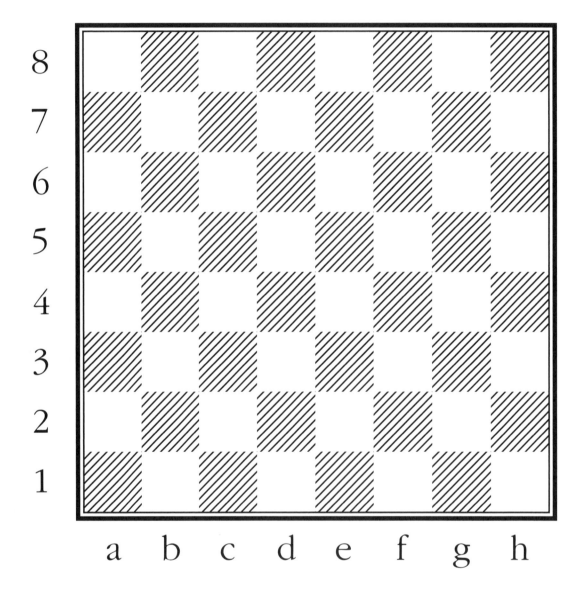

Official Mensa
Game Book

MENSA GUIDE
TO
chess

30
days
to
great
chess

Burt
Hochberg

Sterling Publishing Co., Inc.
New York

For Carol, always
And for Robert, always remembered

Mensa and the distinctive table logo are trademarks of
American Mensa, Ltd. (in the U.S.),
British Mensa, Ltd. (in the U.K.),
Australian Mensa, Inc. (in Australia),
and Mensa International Limited (in other countries)
and are used by permission.

Mensa as an organization does not express an opinion as being that
of Mensa or have any ideological, philosophical, political or religious
affiliations. Mensa specifically disclaims any responsibility for any
liability, loss or risk, personal or otherwise, which is incurred as a
consequence, directly or indirectly, of the use and application of
any of the contents of this book.

Library of Congress Cataloging-in-Publication Data

Hochberg, Burt.
 Mensa guide to chess : 30 days to great chess / Burt Hochberg ; fore-
word by Bruce Pandolfini.
 p.   cm.
"Official Mensa Game Book."
Includes index.
ISBN 0-8069-1241-3
1. Chess. I. Title.
GV1446.H55   2003
794.1—dc22

                                   2003017381

        4 6 8 10 9 7 5 3

Published by Sterling Publishing Co., Inc.
387 Park Avenue South, New York, NY 10016
© 2003 by Burt Hochberg
Distributed in Canada by Sterling Publishing
℅ Canadian Manda Group, 165 Dufferin Street,
Toronto, Ontario, Canada M6K 3H6
Distributed in Great Britain by Chrysalis Books Group PLC
The Chrysalis Building, Bramley Road, London W10 6SP, England
Distributed in Australia by Capricorn Link (Australia) Pty. Ltd.
P.O. Box 704, Windsor, NSW 2756, Australia

Sterling ISBN 0-8069-1241-3

For information about custom editions, special sales, premium and
corporate purchases, please contact Sterling Special Sales
Department at 800-805-5489 or specialsales@sterlingpub.com.

CONTENTS

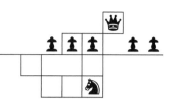

FOREWORD by Bruce Pandolfini

I joined *Chess Life* magazine as a columnist during a chessic gold rush. Bobby Fischer's great successes had just culminated in his capturing the world championship from Russia's Boris Spassky at Reykjavik, Iceland, in 1972, and for chess writers, there was more than enough to write about.

The game's most outstanding writers and columnists—Paul Keres, Lubosh Kavalek, Pal Benko, Svetozar Gligoric, Larry Evans, Robert Byrne, Andy Soltis, Edmar Mednis—were producing stellar work for America's leading chess periodical. *Chess Life* provided everything any chess fan could want, including the latest news, informative reviews, essays on culture and history, stimulating puzzles, annotated games, tournament listings and results, and, of course, state-of-the-art theory. But amid all of that gold there was one indispensable element: Burt Hochberg, the man who put it all together. He was simply the best editor the magazine ever had.

Now Burt has instilled his much-admired expertise and vast experience into his latest book, *Mensa Guide to Chess*. Rules, notation, principles, advice, concrete examples, humor, history, and revealing analyses make Burt's presentation of the royal game one of the most effective and enjoyable anywhere.

As always, Burt is straightforward and thorough. Yet, though he covers all the essentials with marvelous clarity, Burt isn't satisfied with the status quo. Instead of relying on the typically prosaic sequence, where the same ideas follow each other in countless introductory manuals, Burt forges his own path right from the start.

Take the way he introduces notation, which appears much earlier than in so many other comparable texts. Burt turns that early appearance into a distinct advantage, using it to explore his themes fluidly and with far greater precision. Furthermore, he doesn't just parrot the rest of the flock, limiting his discussion to algebraic notation. Descriptive notation has its place, too, so Burt makes sure to explain its application as well. As usual, completeness is his aim.

Burt is also willing to tackle a more advanced concept much earlier than customary—if that's when it applies. His method succeeds, and it succeeds beautifully, because Burt's criteria rest on simple logic. If an idea fits naturally into context, why shouldn't it be explored right then and there, even if that means a challenge for the reader? After all, the best instruction is active instruction, with the student interacting with the material.

To that end, Burt is not interested in satisfying a formula but rather in offering what actually works. And he makes it work by virtue of an engaging narrative that invites the reader to revel in the unfolding plot. Each section flows smoothly into the next, linked by clear explanations, reinforcing examples, review quizzes, illuminating forays into specific subjects, sparkling anecdotes, historical digressions—all crafted with Burt's delightfully reflective and diverting wit.

Sometimes Burt's humor hinges on a slightly altered proverb, such as "do unto others before they can do unto you." Sometimes it comes as a surprise, by virtue of an unexpected analogy: "If you assume that pawns are male, the pawn's ability to become a queen makes chess the only game to include transsexuals." And sometimes it stems from the way Burt gathers and presents his thinking—for example, grouping a set of defining selections from quaint old tomes that ostensibly explain how the knight moves—texts that make you wonder how any real knight ever managed to play a game of chess. But that's Burt. He uses humor to lighten and enhance the learning process, and when he gets a laugh he almost always conveys some useful insight.

Then there's Burt's treatment of chess history. He doesn't just toss in a few isolated facts from the past for reference or to impress. He realizes that relevance and historical perspective are cardinal to true understanding. In *Mensa Guide to Chess* they act in tandem as connective tissue between concepts. Chess authors tend to name a rule, recite it, and move on. But give an exploration into its origin, as Burt does here, and a framework to grasp why and how it developed, and you render the rule much more vivid and therefore memorable. No student who reads this book will need a second account of *en passant*. Burt gives us the why, and that's the best way to learn how.

The book supplies a stream of edifying sidebars, especially on the language of the game. A number of the most confusing chess terms are accordingly given life and color, with analysis of their derivation. These sections especially, with their survey of Spanish, French, German, Italian, Yiddish, and Russian words, show how truly international chess is. Combined with so many details about actual chess history, these passages confer a sense of the game's evolution and primal place in world culture.

Burt also includes plenty of salient quotes from the game's leading exponents (and gives credit where credit is due). Neither is he afraid to mention other texts, even competing ones, if he thinks they can complement his description or help the reader comprehend more. This I found very refreshing, particularly in a discipline known for self-glorification and intellectual stinginess. In fact, I couldn't quite think of any other chess book made of such bone-and-blood integrity and honest gumption.

Mensa Guide to Chess is an excellent introductory chess book, which can be read by virtually any chess enthusiast with profit. Beginners can read it to learn quickly and compellingly. Experienced amateurs can turn to it for review and clarification. Teachers can tap into it to find better ways to explain and impart ideas. And even strong players can read it because it's just plain entertaining. It's simply a good read, even on second and third readings, and this I can say from having read it several times.

PREFACE

Confused?

Chess is too confusing. All those different moves, all those finicky rules, all that heavy thinking, all that stress. It's just too much.

That attitude is what scares a lot of people away from chess. Too bad for them! Their problem is that they're looking at chess the wrong way and not seeing it for what it is.

Chess is a game of *logic and common sense*. Once you learn the moves and the rules, you can see how everything works together and can appreciate its beauty and underlying simplicity.

Chess was developed and refined by innumerable players and theorists over several millennia and in all world cultures. It shares with a very few other ancient board games— go, shogi, and xiang xi (Chinese chess)—a level of refinement and balance that has made it one of the most played games in world history. And its popularity is increasing every day, especially among children.

You don't have to be a genius to play chess. Children as young as five play in scholastic tournaments (for example, in the 2001 Interscholastic Championship tournament in Kansas City, more than *six thousand* children participated). If ordinary five-year-olds can play chess, anybody can. All you need are the logic and common sense that came as standard equipment with your brain.

This book is organized in two sections. The first section introduces the moves and the rules. At the end of the section you will find some exercise positions to test your knowledge. The second section covers the play of the game, where you will learn about tactics and strategy. This section, too, is followed by exercises, a bit more difficult than those that follow the first section. The answers to all exercises are at the end of the book.

By the way, many exercises do not necessarily conform to the order of the material in the book. If they did, you would have a valuable clue to help you solve them. You're not so lucky. Their randomness lets you approach each position as if it were an actual game.

CHESS NOTATION

There are several ways to keep track of the moves of a chess game. These methods also allow you to play over games in books and magazines, to work on solving studies and problems, and to help you teach others to play.

The two major systems are algebraic notation and descriptive notation. The algebraic system, used in Germany and other countries for a couple of centuries, has in recent years become the preferred system in the United States and can now be said to be the dominant system worldwide. It is the system used in this book.

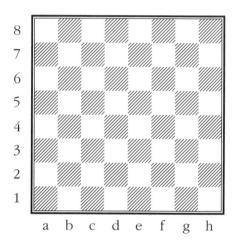

ALGEBRAIC NOTATION

Chess is played on a board made up of 64 squares arrayed in an 8×8 grid of alternately colored squares. In algebraic notation, seen in the empty diagram above right, the letters along the bottom identify the vertical columns (files) from *a* through *h*. The numbers along the left side identify the horizontal rows (ranks) from *1* through *8*. Each individual square is a unique combination of letter and number. The square c4, for example, is the fourth square from the bottom and the third square from the left.

To record a move, simply write the letter identifying the moving piece (K for king, Q for queen, R for rook, B for bishop, and N for knight) and the square it's moving to; for example, Nf3 means a knight move to the square f3. A pawn move is recorded by naming only the square it is moving to with no accompanying letter; thus 1 e4 e5 2 Nf3, etc.

Castling is recorded by either 0-0 (castling on the kingside, the files e-h) or 0-0-0 (castling on the queenside, the files a-d). A capture is indicated by the letter x between the capturing man and the square on which the capture takes place; e.g., Bxc3.

DESCRIPTIVE NOTATION

The descriptive system is fast becoming completely superseded by algebraic notation. In order to read older chess literature, however, it's necessary to know how this system works.

Each square has two names, depending on whether you refer to it from the White or the Black perspective. These names derive from the pieces that stand on them at the beginning of the game. For example, the dark square in the lower left of the diagram is QR1 because the queen rook started there and it is on White's first rank. That square, from Black's perspective, is called QR8 (see diagram at right).

QR8	QN8	QB8	Q8	K8	KB8	KN8	KR8
QR7	QN7	QB7	Q7	K7	KB7	KN7	KR7
QR6	QN6	QB6	Q6	K6	KB6	KN6	KR6
QR5	QN5	QB5	Q5	K5	KB5	KN5	KR5
QR4	QN4	QB4	Q4	K4	KB4	KN4	KR4
QR3	QN3	QB3	Q3	K3	KB3	KN3	KR3
QR2	QN2	QB2	Q2	K2	KB2	KN2	KR2
QR1	QN1	QB1	Q1	K1	KB1	KN1	KR1

From left to right on the first rank, in White's view, the squares are QR1, QN1, QB1, Q1, K1, KB1, KN1, and KR1. The second rank squares, from left to right, are QR2, QN2, QB2, and so on. The third-rank squares are QR3, QN3, QB3, etc.

QR1	QN1	QB1	Q1	K1	KB1	KN1	KR1
QR2	QN2	QB2	Q2	K2	KB2	KN2	KR2
QR3	QN3	QB3	Q3	K3	KB3	KN3	KR3
QR4	QN4	QB4	Q4	K4	KB4	KN4	KR4
QR5	QN5	QB5	Q5	K5	KB5	KN5	KR5
QR6	QN6	QB6	Q6	K6	KB6	KN6	KR6
QR7	QN7	QB7	Q7	K7	KB7	KN7	KR7
QR8	QN8	QB8	Q8	K8	KB8	KN8	KR8

However, White's first rank is, for Black, the eighth rank. So those squares are QR8, QN8, and so on. As you can see, this can be confusing. Descriptive notation is useful for reading older chess books and magazines.

A move is described by naming the moving piece and the square it's moving to; for instance, N-KB3 (Nf3 in algebraic) is a move by a knight to the square KB3. That same move, as seen by Black, is N-KB6.

Pawn moves start with the letter P; for example, 1 P-K4 P-QB4 2 N-KB3 P-Q3 3 P-Q4, etc. Note that QB4 (c5 in algebraic) is on Black's fourth rank, White's fifth.

Castling is as in algebraic. Capturing is a little different. A capture is described by naming the capturing piece and the piece being captured, thus: 1 P-K4 P-K4 2 P-Q4 PxP 3 QxP, and so on.

CHESS IN A NUTSHELL

You probably can't wait to get your hands on the pieces and start moving them around. But before you do, read these first pages; I think you'll find them useful.

A (VERY) LITTLE HISTORY

Chess is really old, so old that nobody knows for sure when and where it originated. Most authorities believe that the game's earliest antecedents developed in China before A.D. 600, probably even earlier. The basic rules of chess as we know them were set down in Europe just before 1500.

Some of the earlier forms of the game that evolved into chess were known by their Persian and Arabic names, *chaturanga* and *shatranj*. These games resembled the modern game only distantly. And in the remote past, long before those games were noticed by historians, what we now call chess may not have been a game at all but rather a common way to diagram battlefield strategy and tactics, like a primitive precursor of the Pentagon Situation Room. Imagining field commanders in days of old planning tactics by moving little armies around on a map helps us to appreciate the unique heritage of this immemorial game.

As the centuries passed and the nature of war changed, so did chess. It migrated in several forms from China and India to Persia and the Arab lands and then to Europe and the New World. It always retained its funda-mental original character: a simulated battle between two armies, exactly what it is today.

THE FORCES

Chess is a game for two players. Each opponent starts with exactly the same forces: sixteen men made up of eight pawns and eight pieces. These men are the somewhat abstract descendants of the military elements actually used when the early forms of chess developed. Pawns represent infantry; knights are soldiers on horseback representing the cavalry; rooks represent chariots (I'll explain later why they look like castle turrets); and bishops, identifiable by their miters, represent the clergy, which was politically very powerful in the Europe of 1500 when the modern rules were set down. And of course there's the royal couple, the king and queen.

One player has the White men, the other the Black. They're always called White and Black no matter what light and dark contrasting colors you may be using.

The battle is fought on a board eight squares wide by eight squares deep. The board is always set up with a light square in each player's near-right corner. The half of the board on which the queens begin the game is the "queenside"—that is, the files (columns) *a* through *d* as shown in the diagram on the next page. The other half is the "kingside"—the files *e* through *h*. The numbers *1* through *8* running up the side of the board identify the eight ranks (horizontal rows). Combine any letter with any number to get the location of any square. This simple "algebraic" system is needed for recording and reading the moves of a game. Algebraic notation is used in this book and in virtually all modern chess books, magazines, newspaper columns, and Web sites. You may still find the older "descriptive" system (explained on page 11) in some old chess literature.

The diagrams always show White at the bottom and Black at the top. The White pawns move up the board, the Black pawns move down.

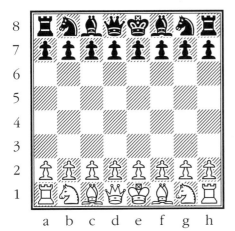

The two sides lined up for battle. The files a–d constitute the queenside; the files e–h make up the kingside. The numbers identify the eight ranks.

The White pieces are lined up on the first rank, the pawns directly in front of them. The Black pieces and pawns are lined up on the seventh and eighth ranks. From left to right, the pieces are rook, knight, bishop, queen, king, bishop, knight, and rook.

MOVING AND CAPTURING

Each different kind of man—king, queen, rook, bishop, knight, and pawn—moves in a unique way. You may move a man either to an empty square or to a square occupied by an opponent's man, thereby capturing it. The captured man is permanently removed from the game. Capturing is always optional unless there's no other legal move. Pieces capture the same way they move, but pawns move and capture in different ways. There is no jumping in chess. In the following chapters, the moves of the pieces and pawns are described in more detail.

• The king moves one square in any direction. It may not move to a square under attack by an enemy man or adjacent to the enemy king. Each king may "castle" once in a game. In castling, the king moves two squares toward one of its own rooks, and the rook moves to the adjacent square on the other side of the king. These two moves are performed as part of the same turn.

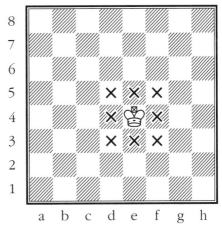

The king can move to any square marked x.

- The queen moves any distance along any unobstructed line in any direction.

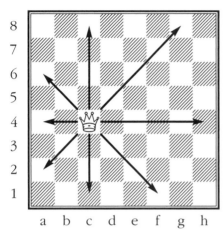

The queen can move any distance along the lines shown.

- The rook moves any distance along any unobstructed line in any horizontal or vertical direction.

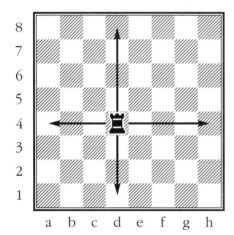

The rook can move to any square along its line of movement.

- The bishop moves any distance along any unobstructed line in any diagonal direction. Each bishop is restricted to the color of the square it starts on.

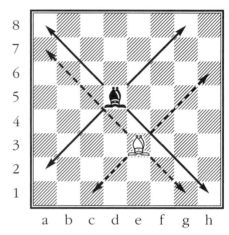

The bishops are limited to the color square they start on. Bishops of opposite colors can never meet.

- The knight moves a distance of exactly two squares: one square diagonally and one square vertically or horizontally in the same general direction, *always landing on the opposite color square.* Its move is not obstructed by anything in its path, and it may not stop at any intervening square.

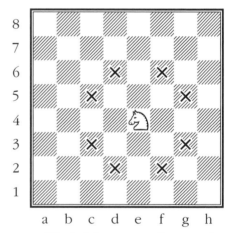

The knight moves a distance of exactly two squares, combining a diagonal and a vertical or horizontal move.

- All pieces (but not pawns) capture the same way they move, by going to a square occupied by an opponent's man and displacing it.

HOW THE PAWNS MOVE AND CAPTURE

- Pawns move straight ahead when advancing but diagonally forward when capturing. Pawns never move backward or sideways.
- Each pawn, on its first move only, may advance either one or two squares straight ahead.
- After its first move, a pawn may advance only one square.
- A pawn may not advance if the square directly in front of it is occupied, but it may capture diagonally if a capture is available.
- A pawn captures by moving one square diagonally forward, replacing the captured enemy man.
- When a pawn is on its fifth rank and an enemy pawn on an adjacent file tries to move past it by advancing two squares, that enemy pawn may be captured "en passant" ("in passing"), as if it had moved only one square.
- When a pawn reaches its last rank it is promoted to any other piece of the same color. It may not remain a pawn or become another king.

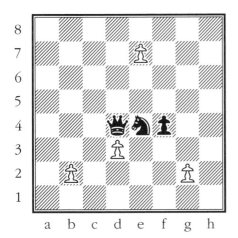

The White pawn on b2 has not yet moved and so can advance either one or two squares. The pawn on d3 can capture the Black knight. It can't move forward because the Black queen is in the way. If the White pawn on e7 advances to e8 it must be promoted to another piece. If the White pawn on g2 advances two squares, it may be captured "en passant" by the Black pawn on f4.

THE OBJECT OF THE GAME

Checkmate! When you directly attack (check) the enemy king and it cannot escape, and your opponent can't capture the attacking man or block the attack, the king is checkmated. The game is over at that point and you have won (the king is never actually captured). In tournaments, the winner scores one point, the loser zero.

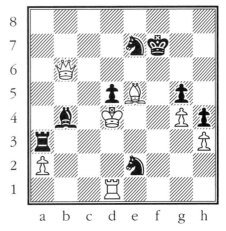

The White king is checkmated by the Black knight on e2.

Checkmate is not the only way to win. In fact it's not often seen in master chess. If you have a great material disadvantage, for instance, and you're very sure you won't be able to recover, you should resign. This is simply an acknowledgment that your opponent will checkmate you eventually. It's no fun to drag out a hopeless game, and there is no shame in resigning. In fact, it's considered poor sportsmanship *not* to resign in a hopeless position. Psychologically, it's better to start a new game than to suffer through one that you know you will lose sooner or later.

DRAWS

A draw is neither a win nor a loss for either player. In competition, each player of a drawn game earns half a point.

There are several ways to draw a game.

AGREEMENT

When both players believe the game is completely equal and without winning chances, or if neither player wants to risk losing by attempting to win, they can call it a draw.

INSUFFICIENT MATERIAL

Certain endgames can't be won because neither player has enough material to force checkmate even if the opponent plays stupidly. A single pawn is theoretically enough to win because it might be promoted. But a lone knight or bishop, with no pawns on the board, is not enough to win. The minimum material needed to force checkmate, with no pawns, is a rook.

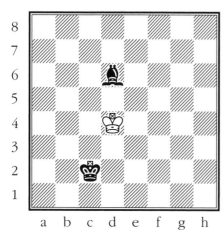

This is a draw due to insufficient mating material. No matter how badly White plays, Black will never be able to checkmate him.

STALEMATE

Another type of draw is stalemate. This situation results when a player has no legal move and his king is *not* in check. If it *is* in check and he has no legal move, it's checkmate.

White to move.

White has a huge material advantage and should checkmate Black in a few moves by playing Kd3 followed by Ke4, Kf5, and Kf6 (or Kg6), bringing up the king to support the queen. But he figures it would be a good idea first to cut off the enemy king's escape by playing Qf7. This is a lousy idea, since the White queen is already confining the Black king to its first rank.

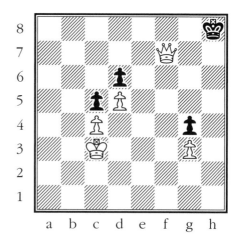

Stalemate! It's Black's turn but he can't move anything and his king is not in check. The game is a draw instead of a win for White. Pity.

THREEFOLD REPETITION

The game is a draw when the same position is repeated (or is about to be repeated) three times with the same player on the move. One form of this is known as perpetual check. It results when one player repeatedly checks the enemy king, which has no way to avoid the checks.

THE THREE PHASES

A game of chess typically consists of three phases: opening, middlegame, and endgame. Although each phase has its own distinguishing characteristics, it often isn't easy to say precisely when one ends and the other begins.

THE OPENING

Your main objectives in the opening:

- Occupy or control center squares by advancing one or two (sometimes three) pawns to the center.
- Develop (mobilize) your pieces quickly, knights before bishops, to fortify the center.
- Bring your king to shelter *away* from the center.

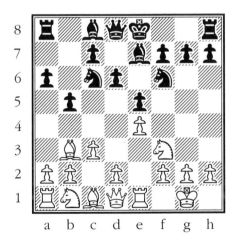

This position arises early in the Ruy Lopez opening. White is preparing to play his pawn from d2 to d4 to occupy more of the center; Black, after moving his knight from c6, will attack White's center with c7-c5.

THE MIDDLEGAME

This phase generally begins when all or most of the pieces have been developed (moved off their starting squares) and the kings have been safely hustled away from the central files. Those files are needed for the rooks. Your objectives in the middlegame:

- Fight for control of the center and other squares that become important as the game develops.
- Bring your pieces into active positions—knights in or near the center, rooks and bishops on open lines (files and diagonals), especially the lines that bear on the center.
- Try to exchange your inactive pieces for your opponent's most active ones.
- Look for ways to build an attack against the enemy king while preserving the safety of your own.
- Try to gain a material advantage.
- Try to get a potential passed pawn on one wing (see page 43).
- Attack your opponent's weak pawns and occupy weak squares in his position.

Although you should always be alert to attacking opportunities—for *both* sides!—you should also strive to avoid weaknesses and prepare for the coming endgame.

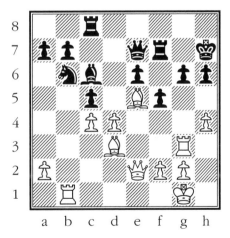

White has a strong attack against the king. Four White pieces (queen, rook, and both bishops) threaten the king's position, already weakened by pawn advances, while only three Black pieces (queen, rook, and king) defend it. In effect, White is a piece up where it matters.

THE ENDGAME

After many or most of the pieces, usually including the queen, have died in battle and there is little opportunity for direct attack against the king, the endgame has arrived.

But why study the endgame, you may ask? Simply checkmate your opponent in the middlegame and you don't *need* the endgame!

Just kidding. Really. Although it would be great to mate your opponent in the middlegame, you can't count on doing so.

First, *always* assume that your opponent will find the best moves. This will help you avoid the temptation of making reckless attacking moves in the hope that your opponent won't see your threats.

Second, trying to force a win when your position doesn't justify direct attack is a fool's errand.

Third, it can be a fatal mistake to think that having achieved a middlegame advantage means you have already won the game. Suppose you get a winning advantage but your opponent stubbornly refuses to give up, forcing you to play out the endgame. What then? Do you know how to win the endgame? Obviously, you need to know the basic endgames just as well as you know the basic openings.

In the endgame the values of the long-range pieces—rooks and bishop—increase because there are fewer pawns and pieces in their way, the king comes out of hiding to become a strong fighting piece, and the remaining pawns finally come into their own.

Your objectives in the endgame:
- With the king no longer in danger of being checkmated, mobilize it by moving it toward the center. The king is a strong piece in the endgame!
- If you have a passed pawn, use your king and other pieces to escort it to the last rank

where it can be promoted. If you don't have a passed pawn, create one!
- If your opponent has a passed pawn, stop it from advancing.

This basic endgame is known as the Lucena position. White can win—if he knows how! See page 103.

THE ELEMENTS

These are the five elements of chess:
- king safety
- material (force)
- space
- time (development)
- pawn structure

KING SAFETY

Among these elements, wrote Reuben Fine in his classic book *The Middle Game in Chess,* "[F]irst place must of course be given to the placement of the king. When it is endangered, nothing else counts." King safety is facilitated by the handy castling maneuver.

MATERIAL

This means pieces and pawns. The player with more material, even as little as one extra pawn, is favored to win the game. But although material is very important, it must be considered together with the other elements. A material advantage alone is no guarantee of a win!

SPACE

The more territory you control, the better. Having more space lets you maneuver your pieces more freely, and this allows you to make threats, build up attacks, and keep your opponent on the defensive.

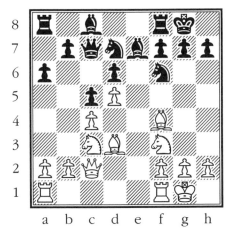

White has such great advantages in space and development that Black can hardly make a useful move.

TIME

This refers especially to the efficiency with which you mobilize your forces in the opening. You should advance one or two pawns to the center to free your pieces, then develop your knights and bishops toward the center. Making unnecessary pawn moves or moving already developed pieces before your development is complete wastes time. Grandmaster Svetozar Gligoric wrote, in the book *How to Open a Chess Game,* "Each move is a treasure, to be spent only in the most useful way." And world champion José Raúl Capablanca, in his book *Chess Fundamentals,* wrote: "I wish to lay stress on the following point which the student should bear in mind. *Before development has been completed no piece should be moved more than once, unless it is essential in order to obtain either material advantage or to secure freedom of action."* (Capablanca's italics.)

In the diagram above, White has advantages in both space and time. All of his pieces are mobilized and his rooks are ready to shift to the central files. Black's rooks and other pieces remain undeveloped. This means that White can make active threats, forcing Black to defend and create weaknesses in his position. In chess terms, White has the "initiative."

PAWN STRUCTURE

Although pawns are the weakest units on the board, each pawn has the potential to become a queen, the strongest piece. Make it one of your top priorities to create at least one potential passed pawn.

Pawns are important in other ways, too. The layout of pawns after the opening (known as the pawn structure or skeleton) marks the space controlled by each player as well as the areas still in dispute. The pawn structure also helps to determine the best places for the pieces. The great attacking genius Rudolf Spielmann wrote: "The pawns are the steel structure of the position and ordinarily dictate the course of events."

Use your pawns to support (protect) your pieces, especially in the center, and to drive away enemy pieces. But try not to let pawns block the open lines that your queen, bishops, and rooks need to work efficiently. Pawns can also be weak targets of attack when they become "isolated," "backward," or "doubled."

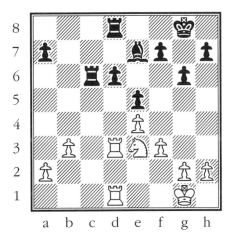

Black's pawn on d6 is "backward" because its neighboring pawns have advanced and can no long protect it. Black is forced to defend it with his pieces, limiting their mobility and preventing him from playing actively.

ANOTHER IMPORTANT ELEMENT

All chess manuals talk about these elements but few, if any, mention another element that is no less important: attitude, or, if you prefer, psychology.

A chess game is a fight, a contest for primacy. The object is to win, not to play nice. The aggressive player who is always making threats wins more often than the cautious, defensive player. This is especially true of beginners and intermediate players. It takes experience to learn how to defend well. We naturally tend to trust our opponents and overestimate their threats. This is why even risky and unsound attacks often succeed against opponents who become intimidated and make panicky or timid moves. In the first decades of the 20th century, the great grandmasters Rudolf Spielmann and Frank Marshall won many games and tournaments

by attacking ferociously and sacrificing pieces. Half a century later, Mikhail Tal became world champion by following the same strategy. Even though some of their sacrifices were dubious, these players understood a psychological truth. As Spielmann put it, "Errors occur far more frequently in defense than in attack."

Always look for good ways to make active threats to keep your opponent on the defensive. But don't be blind to what your opponent is threatening. In chess it pays to be paranoid. Always assume that your opponent is planning something nefarious, and make it your business to see his threats before you make your move.

Don't panic! Learn how to defend yourself calmly and coolly. As in other types of competition, the best defense is often a good offense. If you're attacked, try to find a sound counter-threat instead of defending meekly. Don't be "polite" and hesitate to attack because you think your opponent will be mad at you. He certainly won't hesitate to attack you! To paraphrase an old saying: Do unto others before they can do unto you.

PREPARING FOR BATTLE (And a Little Algebra)

At opposite ends of the battlefield stand two armies poised for war. But unlike real battles, where the generals can set up their forces any way they please, in chess the starting positions of the forces are fixed.

The chessboard is always set up for play with a light square in each player's near right corner. Remember: light on the right.

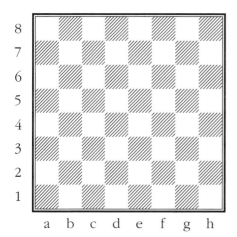

The vertical columns lettered a-h are the files, and the horizontal rows labeled 1-8 are the ranks. Any combination of a letter and a number identifies a unique square on the board. This is the "algebraic" chess notation system, which is used in virtually all chess literature today. (See page 10 for more details on the algebraic system and to learn the old "descriptive" notation system, which is found in older literature and is still used by a few contemporary writers.) This international chess language is a simple and convenient tool that lets you record and play over games and to read chess analysis from all over the world. When looking at the chessboard, try to think in terms of algebraic notation; it will soon become second nature.

Meanwhile, let's assign the pawns and pieces to their starting positions.

The pawns start on each player's second rank—White's a2 to h2, Black's a7 to h7. In all the diagrams in this book, White is at the bottom, Black at the top. White moves up the board, Black moves down.

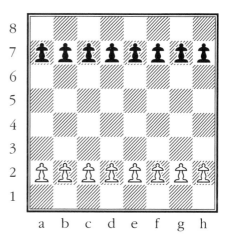

The pieces line up behind their pawns. The kings and queens (abbreviated K and Q in chess notation) start on the central files—the kings on the e-file, the queens on the d-file. Remember that the queen takes its own color—the White queen on a light square, the Black queen on a dark square. The kings and queens, like the other pieces, face each other across the battlefield.

For convenience in discussing chess strategy and tactics, the half of the board on which the queens start—the files *a* through *d*—is called the queenside; the other half—the files *e* through *h*—is called the kingside.

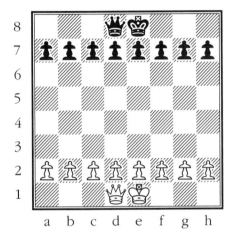

The rooks (abbreviated R) go in the corners.

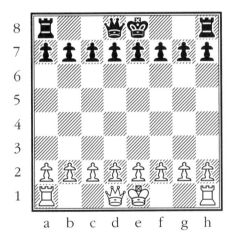

The knights (abbreviated N; the letter K is reserved for the king) stand next to the rooks:

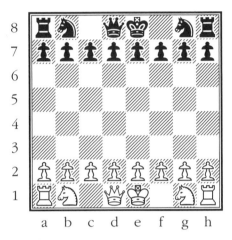

Finally, the bishops (abbreviated B) cozy up to the royals:

NOW IT BEGINS ...

Study this position carefully! If you've read the introductory chapter, "Chess in a Nutshell," you already have some idea of how the game works. The following chapters explain the moves and the strategy and tactics of chess in more detail. For now, just look at the diagram—better yet, set up your own board and men—and, without touching anything, try to visualize the shape of the battle to come. Try to feel the power of the pieces.

You and your opponent will advance central pawns to take control of as much of the center as you can. You will mobilize your knights and bishops to support those pawns, attack your opponent's center pawns, and improve your control of the center. As soon as possible, you will bring your kings to safer ground by castling (see page 27). The castling maneuver will also mobilize one of your rooks. Rooks should occupy central files.

The object of the game is of course to checkmate the enemy king. But this is not a realistic objective at first unless your opponent plays foolishly. Giving away a pawn or two and throwing your strongest pieces wildly across the board before you have completely mobilized your forces is foolish. Such attempts almost always fail against smart players, for the simple reason that they go against the logic of chess.

The best way to train is to play as often as you can, preferably against stronger players, and to study as many master games as you can find. You can view thousands of games by the great masters on the Internet using a convenient and free chess viewer. If you don't have access to the Internet, you can find innumerable master games in books and chess magazines. Play over these games again and again. Don't spend too much time on individual moves at first; you can go back and study them later. Instead, try to appreciate how the game flows from opening to middlegame to endgame and how the players' plans evolve. Note especially how the players fight for control of central squares throughout the game.

CHANGE THE RULES?

The starting position in chess is the same as it was roughly 700 years ago, despite many efforts to change it. The most frequent attempts have been to switch one side's king and queen or both sides' bishops and knights. Both of these alterations have the effect of negating much opening theory.

The most interesting suggestion, and recently the most closely examined by some important players, is a random or unfixed opening setup. In a variant called "shuffle" chess (blessed by Bobby Fischer and of course by all of his acolytes), a computer decides where the pieces stand behind their pawns. The players have no say in this and don't start thinking until all the pieces are in place. This makes it almost impossible for a player to prepare an opening strategy before the game starts, as they do in orthodox chess.

In another "unfixed" method (which has no universally approved name), the game begins with only the pawns on the board; the players alternately place their pieces wherever they like behind their pawns, one by one, starting with the king. With this method, the players start thinking strategically even before the pieces are on the board.

If you're interested in chess variants, you'll find a zillion of them on the Internet at www.chessvariants.com.

A NOTE ON NOTATION

See those little numbers and letters bordering each diagram? They're used in algebraic notation to identify the ranks (horizontal rows), files (vertical columns), and individual squares on the board. To locate a square, simply combine a letter with a number. This kind of diagram is helpful for beginning students, but in most chess literature the letters and numbers are omitted

Algebraic chess notation comes in two sizes, long and abbreviated. In long algebraic, a move is described by identifying the piece being moved, the square it's moving from, and the square it's moving to. Abbreviated algebraic, which is used in this book and most others, omits the departure square. Once you know the name of the moving piece and where it's going, the departure square is superfluous. Say you're moving a knight from g1 to f3. This move can be notated simply as Nf3. You don't need to specify that it's moving from g1 unless more than one knight can move to f3.

One of the best chess teachers is the computer. A good chess program will brutally punish your mistakes so you won't make them again.

The next chapters will explain the moves of the pieces and pawns, and then we'll see how to put all that pent-up energy to work in practice.

2

HOW THE KING MOVES AND CAPTURES

The king is the one indispensable piece and the ultimate focus of all the comings and goings on the board. For most of the game the king is relatively weak and needs to be sheltered and guarded by its army. But in the endgame, when there are few pieces on the board and the king can safely venture out into the open, it's a very strong piece.

The king moves one square in any of the eight possible directions. But it may not move to a square that is under attack by an enemy man or next to the enemy king. It can capture any unprotected man on any square to which it can move. It cannot, however, capture a protected man, because that would place the king in check, which is illegal.

Neither king can move to any of the three squares between them (e3, e4, and e5). Black's king can't move to c4 because that square is controlled by the White pawn. But he can capture that pawn because it's not protected.

The king is highly allergic to being attacked. When a king is checked (directly attacked), it must get out of check immediately, on the very next move. Every man in its army, from lowly pawn to mighty queen, must be ready to give up its life to save the king. The life of the king takes precedence over everything else. If the king is checkmated—that is, if it can't move out of check, block the attack, or capture the attacker—the game is over.

Check and checkmate are further explained on page 46.

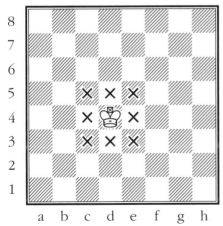

The king can move to any marked square.

In deference to the royal personage of the king, special rules apply to the preservation of its life and safety:

- It is illegal to move your king into check; that is, to a square attacked by an enemy man.
- It is illegal to expose your king to attack by moving a man that is "pinned" against it. (See page 77 for an explanation of pin.)
- It is illegal to move your king next to the enemy king.
- Each king, once in a game, may "castle," a maneuver in which the king and a rook both move in the same turn to bring the king away from the center. See the next chapter, "Castling: A Special King Move."

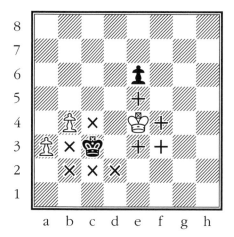

The White king can move to any square marked +. It can't go to d5 or f5 because those squares are guarded by the pawn on e6 (remember: in diagrams Black pawns move *down* the board). The Black king can move to any square marked ×. Taking the pawn on b4 is illegal because the pawn is protected by the other White pawn. Neither king can move to d3 or d4 because those squares are next to the enemy king.

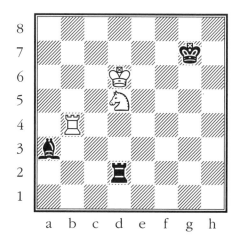

White can't move his rook or knight because either move would illegally expose his king to attack. Those two pieces are "pinned."

THE LANGUAGE OF CHESS

Chess gets its name from its biggest VIP, the king. In ancient Persia, where one of the antecedents of modern chess developed, the word for king was *shah*. From this word, still used in modern times, the word for chess in many languages was derived: *Schach* (German), *skak* (Swedish, pronounced "shahk"), *shakhmaty* (Russian), *échecs* (French), *scacchi* (Italian, pronounced "shahky"), *sakk* (Hungarian, pronounced "shahk"), and others. That Persian word was also the basis for *shatranj* and *chaturanga*, the names of the two major forerunners of modern chess.

3

CASTLING: A Special King Move

King safety is a fundamental priority of chess strategy, along with rapid development, control of the center, and sound pawn structure. Losing the king loses the game, so it's vital to make sure early on, before the battle heats up and the bullets start flying, that the king is snug in its castle, away from the action and protected by its army.

The laws of chess give each king a once-in-a-lifetime opportunity to move from its vulnerable starting position to a relatively safe place. This maneuver is called castling.

Castling is the only time when two pieces are allowed to move in the same turn. It's the biggest bargain in chess. Castling accomplishes two important goals.

First: The king is not safe where it begins the game. When you advance your middle pawns to free your pieces, you leave your king somewhat exposed. Castling takes your king away from that and moves it to a safe corner.

Second: Castling moves a rook out of the corner and to a central file, and connects the two rooks on the first rank. Rooks work best when they work together.

The castling maneuver involves the king and either of your rooks. The king first slides two squares toward the rook, and then the rook hops to the square adjacent to the king on its other side. In scorekeeping, castling is indicated by 0-0 ("short" castling on the kingside) and 0-0-0 ("long" castling on the queenside). The zeroes represent the number of squares the rook passes over—two squares when castling short, three squares when castling long.

LOOKING BACK

Once upon a time, in *shatranj*, the king could move only one square at a time, as in modern chess but without the ability to castle. An immobile king is pretty much at the mercy of attacking forces. Around the 13th century, chess historians believe, the rules were gradually changed to allow a previously unmoved king to make a two-square leap under certain conditions; from this practice the castling maneuver evolved. The king-rook castling maneuver was fully established by the end of the 16th century.

The White king and rooks where they start the game.

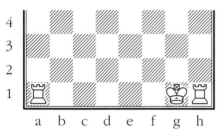

Kingside castling: first the king moves two squares toward the king rook.

Then the rook moves to the other side of the king.

Queenside castling: first the king moves two squares toward the queen rook.

Then the rook moves to the other side of the king.

Special rules apply to castling:

- Each king may castle only once in a game, on either the kingside or the queenside.
- The squares between the king and the castling rook must be unoccupied.
- The squares the king passes over and lands on may not be under attack. This does not apply to the rook.
- The king may not have previously moved (though it may have been previously checked).
- The rook on the castling side may not have previously moved.
- The king may not be in check (that is, it may not castle to get out of check).

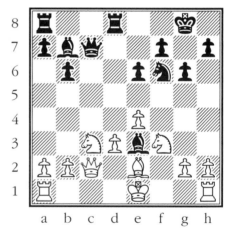

White can't castle on either side now because the black bishop is attacking both c1 and g1.

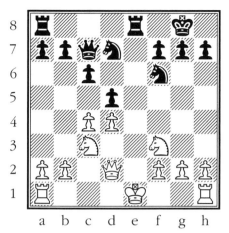

White can't castle now on either side because his king is in check. He may be able to castle later if he gets out of check without moving his king.

Many players, not only beginners, are in a big hurry to start attacking the minute the game starts. Sometimes—for instance when your opponent has made some terrible moves and weakened his position—this strategy may be justified. But usually it's not worth the risk. Take your time. Before thinking about your opponent's king, take a minute to think about your own.

Castling can also be a strong attacking move in the right circumstances. Here's a particularly brutal example, from a 1934 game between Feuer and O'Kelly.

O'Kelly

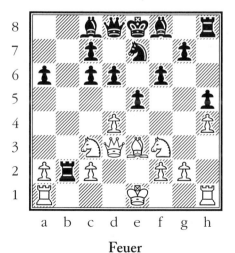

Feuer

The presence of Black's rook on b2 gives White an idea.

White	Black
11 dxe5	

This is played not simply to exchange pawns in the center but also, and more to the point, to force the Black king to the d-file. (The ellipsis below indicates the absence of a White move.)

11 ...	dxe5?
12 Qxd8+	Kxd8

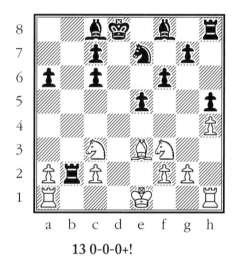

13 0-0-0+!

Surprise! O'Kelly must have forgotten that White could castle, and with check, no less. On the next move White picks up the rook on b2 and sends it to a school for wayward pieces.

4

HOW THE QUEEN MOVES AND CAPTURES

The queen, like the king, can move in any of the eight possible directions. But, unlike the king, it can move any distance. It may capture the first enemy man it encounters along its line of movement.

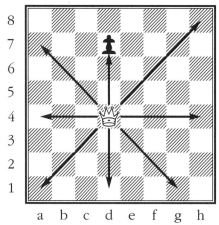

The queen can move to any unoccupied square along the lines shown or can capture the pawn on d7.

The queen is the strongest piece because it has the greatest mobility. Such a powerful weapon must be wielded with care. Never exchange it for a piece of lesser value unless you see an immediate way to win the game or restore the material balance. (See "Chess Family Values," page 66).

Because the queen is so strong, it is an excellent target. If you bring it out too early, it can be harassed by weaker men. If attacked by a weaker man it must retreat, which usually is a loss of time, and time is a valuable commodity in chess.

For instance:

White	Black
1 e4	d5

The Center Counter Defense, as this opening is known, is not recommended for Black unless you really know what you're doing (and your opponent doesn't). If White plays sensibly, Black loses either time or material.

2 exd5	Qxd5

This leads to a loss of time. The queen should not be exposed so early without a very good reason. The following attacks on the queen by White's pieces give White an advantage in development, which in the opening is equivalent to an advantage in time. Black should play 2 ... Nf6 and try to recapture the pawn on d5 later with the knight.

3 Nc3

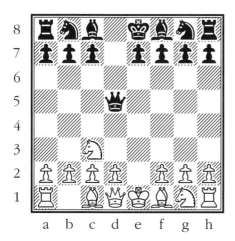

The queen has several possible moves, but White can answer each of them with another developing move. For example, after 3 ... Qd8 4 Nf3 White already has two pieces developed, Black none. Or 3 ... Qa5 4 d4, and White is way ahead in controlling the center.

3 ...   Qe5+

The plus sign indicates check in algebraic notation.

4 Be2

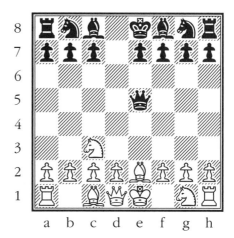

White's next move will be Nf3 or d4. Black's queen will be forced to move yet again, losing more time and leaving White with a big lead in development.

Hang a sign around your queen's crown that says HANDLE WITH CARE!

LOOKING BACK

The queen, now the strongest piece on the board, was once a weak piece with little mobility. (Remember: mobility equals strength.) In *chaturanga* and *shatranj*, two of the ancient games from which chess evolved, the piece that eventually became the queen was the *firzan*, later *fers* (still the word for queen in Russian, pronounced "fairs"). It could move only one square diagonally but could also hop specific distances. In the late 15th century, probably on orders from Queen Isabella of Castile (the same lady who sponsored Christopher Columbus's first voyage to the New World), the chess queen was given vastly greater powers and became a stronger piece even than the king. It's interesting to speculate how chess might have developed if a man instead of a woman had occupied the Castilian throne in those days.

HOW THE ROOK MOVES AND CAPTURES

The rook moves either vertically or horizontally in any of four directions. It moves any distance in an unobstructed straight line. It may capture the first enemy man it encounters.

The rook is the strongest piece on the board besides the queen (see "Chess Family Values," page 66). It's strong because it's mobile: it can travel all the way across the board in a single move and, unlike the bishop, can attack squares of both colors. Like the other long-range pieces—the bishop and queen—it functions best in uncrowded positions. It's particularly strong in the endgame.

Rooks belong on open files—don't smother them! It's important to get both rooks working together by castling and developing all the other pieces.

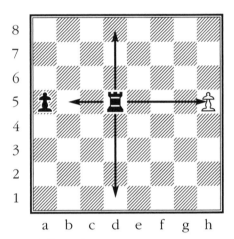

The rook can move to any square along the lines or it can take the white pawn on h5.

THE LANGUAGE OF CHESS

In *chaturanga*, the piece we now know as the rook was a chariot, one of the elements of ancient warfare. The word "rook" is distantly derived from the Sanskrit *ratha* and the Old Persian *rukh*, the word for chariot. When Italian became the predominant language of chess, in the 16th century, the word *rukh* was assimilated as the near homophone *rocco*, the word for tower. In the standard "Staunton" chess set in common use today, the rook has the appearance of a castle tower or turret rather than the chariot sometimes seen in antique chess sets. The Staunton set gets its name from the great English player Howard Staunton, who commissioned the design in the 19th century.

HOW THE BISHOP MOVES AND CAPTURES

A bishop moves any distance in an unobstructed diagonal line in any of four directions. It may capture an enemy man along its line of movement.

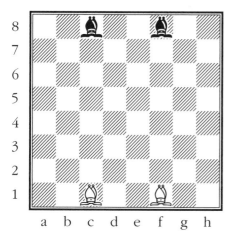

The starting positions of the four bishops.

The bishops on the light squares f1 and c8 in the diagram move only on the light squares, while the bishops on the dark squares c1 and f8 move only on the dark squares. Bishops that travel on opposite-color squares live in parallel worlds, as it were, and can never meet.

Boris Spassky, who won the world championship in 1969 from Tigran Petrosian and lost it to Bobby Fischer in 1972, explained in this way why he and his first wife were divorced: "We were like bishops of opposite colors."

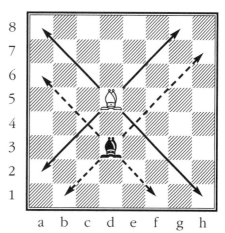

The bishops that start on the light squares are restricted to the light squares throughout the game.

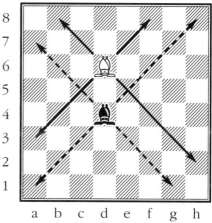

The bishops that start on the dark squares are restricted to the dark squares throughout the game.

Because of their ability to sweep all the way across the board in a single move, bishops are strong pieces, especially in open positions where there are few pieces and pawns on the board. They are less effective in closed or crowded positions because their mobility is reduced. Two bishops together are extremely powerful, and in open positions the so-called bishop-pair can be devastating.

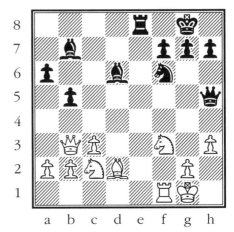

In this more open position with fewer pawns, the bishops, especially the black bishop-pair, have great power.

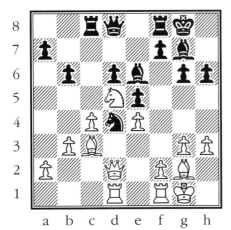

In this closed position with most of the pawns still on the board, the bishops have limited scope.

LOOKING BACK

One of the oddities of chess history is that the modern bishop is actually descended from the elephant. In *shatranj*, the piece that represented that powerful beast of war was the *fil* (the name is preserved in the modern, Arabic-influenced Spanish name for the bishop, *alfil*). The *fil* moved like the modern chess bishop but had much less range. When its power was increased at the end of the 15th century, its appearance suddenly changed to that of a miter—the bifurcated headdress worn by bishops and high priests in several religions—undoubtedly in recognition of the political power then held by the church.

7

HOW THE KNIGHT MOVES AND CAPTURES

Although knights looks like horses (because they represents the cavalry in early forms of the game), they're actually cavaliers and don't like to be called horses.

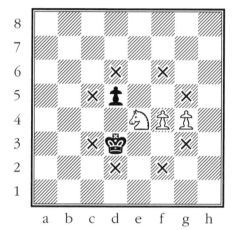

The knight can move to any of the squares shown and has no effect on intervening squares. It moves around any men on neighboring squares.

Unlike the other pieces, the knight doesn't move in a straightforward way. Although its move is generally described as an L-shape—one square horizontally and two squares vertically or vice versa—that definition can be confusing because it adds up to three squares. The knight moves a distance of only *two* squares, never more, never less. The move combines one square diagonally and one square vertically or horizontally in the

same general direction, *always landing on a square of the opposite color,* as shown in the diagram at left. The knight has no effect on any intervening square and has the unique ability to maneuver around or between or through any man or men of either color. This makes the knight particularly useful in crowded positions.

Because the knight's move is a fixed distance of exactly two squares, it normally does not work well at the edge of the board, where its mobility is reduced by half, as shown in the next diagram.

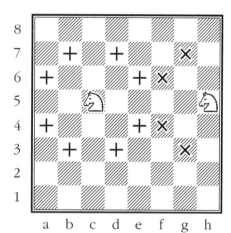

The knight on h5, at the edge of the board, can move to only four squares (marked ×). The knight on c5, near the center, has twice that range (marked +).

35

JUST SAY "NEIGH!"

Describing the knight's move succinctly and accurately can be a challenge. Considering the many different descriptions that have appeared in chess books over the last two hundred years or so, some chess writers seem to have had little faith in their readers' ability to understand a simply stated definition. Just for fun, here are a few examples.

First, the official description in the latest (1997) revision of the Laws of Chess adopted by the International Chess Federation (FIDE): "The knight moves to one of the squares nearest to that on which it stands but not on the same rank, file or diagonal. It does not pass directly over any intervening square." Clear enough.

A more geometric description comes from the second edition (1992) of *The Oxford Companion to Chess*, by David Hooper and Kenneth Whyld: "A move of fixed length from one corner to the diagonally opposite corner of a rectangle three squares by two. It has no fixed route, only a departure and an arrival square." The second sentence means that a knight, unlike a queen, bishop, or rook, may not stop between the square it's moving from and the square it's moving to.

If you're of a mathematical bent, you'll appreciate another definition in a different section of the same book: "[T]he knight is a leaper that is moved a distance $\sqrt{5}$ squares for which the co-ordinates are 1 and 2."

The following chronologically arranged descriptions—I should say, over-descriptions—are taken from some musty old chess manuals. They are technically correct (except the one by Lee and Gossip) but often so confusing that you wonder how anybody managed to learn chess from those books. Certainly they are responsible for the knight's reputation as a "difficult" piece. The hilarious sentence by Young and Howell is a masterpiece of obfuscating prolixity. My word processor's automatic grammar checker had a conniption fit when I typed it and may never forgive me. (These and other definitions of the knight's move were collected by the English chess writer Edward Winter and published on The Chess Café Web site. I thank them for allowing me to hijack this material.)

Stratagems of Chess, by Anonymous (1817): "The knights move obliquely, backward or forward, upon every third square, including that which they stood on, from black to white, and white to black."

The Book of Chess, by G.H. Selkirk (1868): "The knight's move is simply two squares of the rook's move, and then one square at right angles, finishing on the last-mentioned, and having power over it alone."

The Laws and Practice of Chess, by H. Staunton and R. Wormald (1876): "His leap carries him over one square in a straight line to one in an oblique direction. But this peculiarity will be better understood by an attentive study of the annexed diagram, and very much more readily by the tuition of some chess-playing acquaintance." This is a strangely reticent description considering that Howard Staunton was one of the three or four best players of his time and also the world's greatest Shakespearean scholar.

Chess, by L. Hoffer (1892 and other editions): "One move of the knight combines two king's moves: one square straight, and one square diagonally to any but the adjoining squares to its starting-point."

The Principles of Chess in Theory and Practice, by J. Mason (1894 and other editions): "The knight's distance is limited to two squares, and his direction is intermediate between the rectangular one of the rook and diagonal one of the bishop. Mathematically considered, the knight's move is in the diagonal of a rectangle of six squares or points."

The Minor Tactics of Chess, by F.K. Young and E.C. Howell (1895): "We now come to the knight, which radiates its force in the directions of obliques; and as the length of the oblique is fixed and invariable, the magnitude of the force exerted by the knight in any one direction is also fixed and invariable; that is, the knight commands only one point in any one direction, that point being the final point of the oblique of which the position of the knight is the initial point."

Chess for Beginners and the Beginners of Chess, by R.B. Swinton (1897): "The move is from a black square to a white, or from a white square to a black, round the corner, traversing one square diagonally to the next straightforwards; or one square straightforwards to the next diagonally."

The Complete Chess-Guide, by F.J. Lee and G.H.D. Gossip (1914): "The knight moves in a peculiar way, viz., one square diagonally and then one square forwards, backwards, or sideways, or vice versa, one square forwards or backwards or laterally and one square diagonally. His move combines the action of the shortest move of the bishop and the shortest move of the rook, or vice versa." If you try to follow this description by moving an actual knight on an actual board, you will see that "one square diagonally and then one square ... backwards" is wrong.

Confused? Who wouldn't be?

The knight's limited mobility makes it slightly inferior to the bishop in most positions, and much weaker than the rook and queen. A well-placed knight, however—which usually means in or near the center—can be very powerful. And at close range it can be a monster due to its "forking" ability (see page 74).

This is from a game played at a Russian team championship in 1962. White sacrificed his queen a few moves earlier to get a strong attack, which is now in progress. Although his knight can take the Black rook on f7, he has a much better move. (He can't play fxe5 because his f-pawn is pinned.)

Chernikov

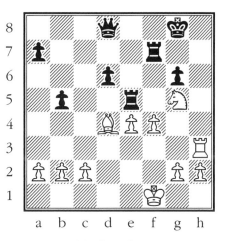

Nezhmedtinov

White to move

1 Rh8+!   Kxh8

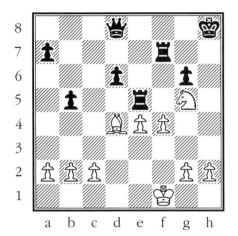

2 Nxf7+

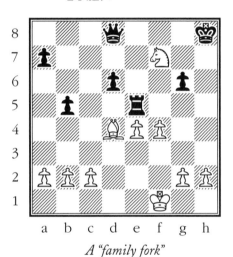

A "family fork"

As pretty a picture as you'll ever see. The knight simultaneously attacks the king, queen, and rook. An attack by a single man on two or more enemy men at the same time is called a fork. This one is a "family fork" because it hits both members of the royal family.

Despite all their advantages, knights can be clumsy, too, requiring at least two moves to get to an adjacent square.

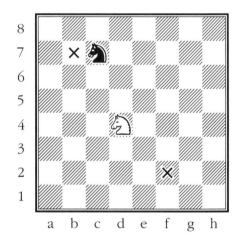

Even though the Black knight on c7 is right next to the square b7, it needs three moves to get there. One possible route is e8-d6-b7. The White knight, though only two squares from f2, can't get there in fewer than four moves; for example, e2-f4-d3-f2.

8

HOW THE PAWN MOVES AND CAPTURES

The pawn is the foot soldier of chess, the unit of lowest value compared to the pieces. Because pawns move only forward, never backward or sideways, they are usually the first units to engage the enemy in battle and often the first casualties.

Pawns are often considered expendable: cannon fodder used to clear lines for attack or to gain time or the initiative. But pawns not only perform necessary tasks both offensively and defensively, each pawn also has within it the seed of a new queen, the most powerful piece on the board.

There are two things to keep in mind about pawns. First, the basic pawn structure, which is for the most part established early on, prefigures the character of the game to come. A blocked, immobile pawn structure usually means a slow, maneuvering tug-of-war, while a flexible pawn structure leads to a more active fight. Second, because the pawn—and only the pawn—has the potential of becoming a queen when it reaches its last square, it has two lives, not just one.

PAWN MOVES

When moving without capturing, a pawn advances straight ahead one square, except on its first move, when it may move either one or two squares. If the square directly in front of a pawn is occupied, the pawn is blocked and can't advance.

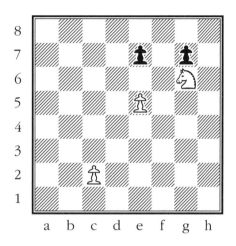

White's pawn on c2 has not yet moved, so it can make its first move to either c3 or c4. But White's pawn on e5, which has already moved at least twice, may advance only one square, to e6.

Black's g7-pawn can't move because the square in front of it is occupied. His pawn on e7, even though it has not yet moved and is entitled to a two-square first move, can advance only one square because the square e5 is occupied.

PAWN CAPTURES

Pawns, unlike pieces, capture differently from the way they move. This is one of several rules obviously invented to bewilder beginners. To capture, a pawn moves one square *diagonally* forward and captures the

THE LANGUAGE OF CHESS

The word "pawn" is derived from the Latin *pes*, foot. From that Latin root we also get "peon," which has several meanings: a foot soldier; an agricultural laborer; a peasant, and an indentured servant. Another derivation from *pes* is "pioneer," which is a pretty good way to think of a pawn. The German word for pawn is *bauer*, which means, among other things, peasant. The Russian word, transliterated as "pyeshka," is related to the Russian word for foot.

enemy man on that square. It does not capture by moving straight ahead.

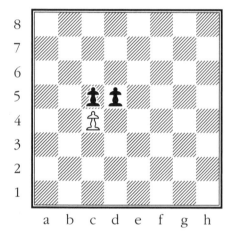

The White pawn on c4 can capture the Black pawn on d5 but not the one on c5.

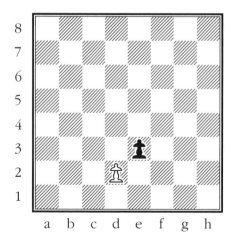

White's pawn on d2 has three options: it can advance one square or two squares or can

take the Black pawn on e3. It cannot both advance and capture on the same turn.

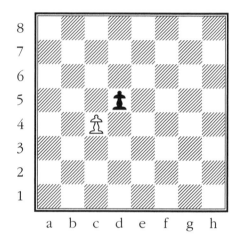

Black's pawn on d5 can either take White's pawn on c4 or advance to d4. If Black plays dxc4, the following position is reached.

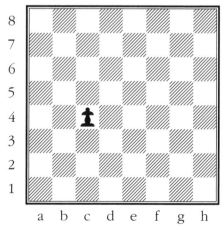

Position after Black has played dxc4.

9

SPECIAL PAWN MOVES

Though pawns have been called the "soul" of chess and have surprising power, they are vexing to many beginners because of the many "fiddly" rules associated with them. In this chapter I'll show you how simple those fiddly rules really are.

EN PASSANT

En passant (pronounced ahn pass-AHNT) means "in passing." It's one of the pawn's neatest tricks. Some beginners find this rule bewildering, but you won't after reading this chapter. (Don't tell anybody, but in some cosmopolitan chess clubs, this maneuver is called "en pissoir." You can guess the meaning.)

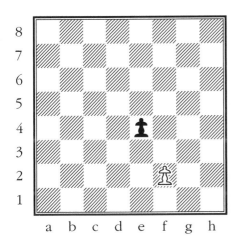

The naked facts about en passant captures:

- The capturing pawn must be on its fifth rank.
- The advancing enemy pawn must be on an adjoining file and must be making its first move, a two-square advance.
- The capturing pawn may take the advancing pawn as if it had advanced only one square.
- En passant captures, like all captures, are optional unless there's no other legal move (see "Check," page 46).
- An en passant capture may be made only on the first opportunity in each case.

White doesn't want to move his f-pawn to f3 because Black could capture it. Since the f-pawn hasn't moved yet, it has the option of advancing two squares. So White plays f2-f4, hoping to sneak it past the Black pawn. But now the en passant rule comes into play:

Position after f2-f4

Black plays exf3 e.p. That is, he takes White's pawn "in passing," as if it had moved only one square. (En passant is abbreviated e.p. in chess notation.)

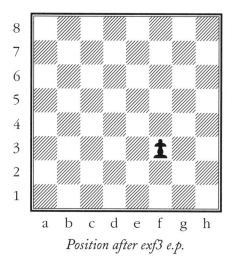

Position after exf3 e.p.

Although the en passant capture is optional, it's a use-it-or-lose-it proposition. If you want to capture en passant you must do so immediately, on the first opportunity. If you pass it up, you will never be able to take that particular pawn en passant (though you can capture it in an ordinary way at any time). Other en passant opportunities may arise with other pawns.

Here's an example.

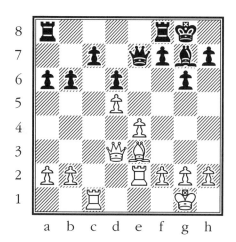

Black is not feeling too happy. White has a powerful position in the center and all his pieces are well posted. Black realizes that his c-pawn is in trouble because it's backward on a half-open file and confronted by an enemy rook. So he decides to eliminate the weak pawn by advancing it two squares.

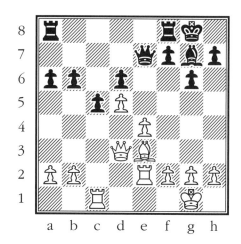

This move looks strong: it removes the weakness on c7 and prepares to gain space on the queenside by advancing the a-pawn, b-pawn, and c-pawn. But it's a terrible blunder because of just one teeny little problem: dxc6 e.p.!

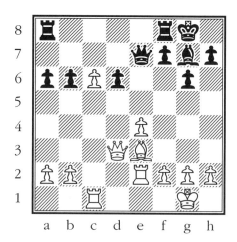

White took Black's pawn "in passing," as if it had advanced one square instead of two. Now Black's position is even worse than before. White has an extra pawn and a passed pawn on c6, while Black's d-pawn is a new weakness, isolated and on an open file.

....
PASSED PAWNS

A pawn has the opportunity to live a second life as a queen or some other piece after reaching its last rank. This gives it enormous reserve power. The mere possibility that the opponent has a *potential* passed pawn—one that might become a passed pawn and eventually a queen—should keep you wide-awake and alert, as if there were a burglar in your house. "The passed pawn is a criminal, who should be kept under lock and key," wrote the grandmaster and theoretician Aron Nimzovich in his influential book *My System*.

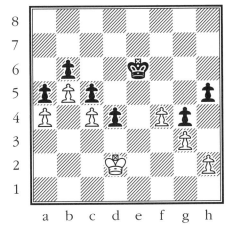

Each side has a passed pawn, White on f4, Black on d4.

A passed pawn is dangerous not only because it is a potential new queen but also because it can't be stopped or captured by enemy pawns, only by pieces. Since an extra queen would be an overwhelming material advantage, the opponent must stop the passed pawn at any cost, even if this means sacrificing a piece. By the way, since a pawn is almost always promoted to the strongest piece—a queen—promotion is commonly called "queening." (If you assume that pawns are male, the pawn's ability to become a queen makes chess the only game to include transsexuals.)

Potential passed pawns develop from certain pawn structures and in other ways. In the diagram below, White does not yet have a passed pawn, but his pawn on c4 is a *potential* passed pawn.

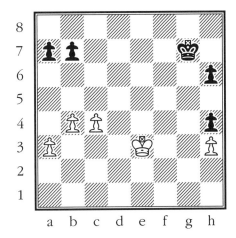

A healthy pawn majority like White's on the queenside should eventually yield a passed pawn. Advancing pawns and trading them one for one on that side will, by simple attrition, leave White with one unopposed queenside pawn.

Now look at the kingside. Black has a two-to-one pawn majority there, but it's impotent because he can't do what White can do on the queenside; that is, produce a passed pawn by advancing pawns and forcing exchanges.

Here's an example from the end of a tournament game.

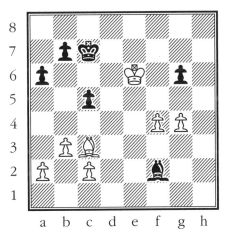

White has a two-to-one pawn majority and a potential passed pawn on the kingside. A simple pawn trade will leave him with one unopposed pawn, which will advance to become a queen. He can play, for instance, f4-f5.

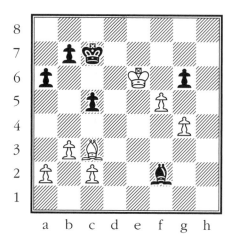

Whatever Black does now, White gets a passed pawn and wins the game. If Black captures, White either recaptures or plays g4-g5. If Black plays g6-g5, White simply marches his pawn to the eighth rank and makes a new queen.

PAWN PROMOTION

- When a pawn reaches its last rank it is immediately promoted, as part of the same move, to a piece of the same color. It may not remain a pawn or become a second king. A pawn reaching the eighth rank *must* be promoted.
- A pawn may be promoted to a queen (or any piece except a king) even if you already have other pieces of the same type. Since you start with eight pawns, you can theoretically have nine queens—the original plus eight promoted pawns.

- The promoted pawn assumes the powers of the new piece immediately.
- A newly promoted piece may give check at the moment it is promoted.
- A pawn may arrive at its last rank by making a capture.

Here's an example illustrating all of the above:

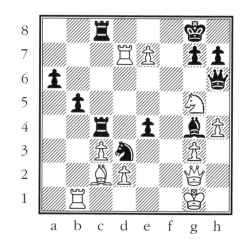

Black has just made a fatal blunder by moving his bishop from h5 to g4, attacking White's rook on d7. White now brings the game to a swift end by playing Rd8+.

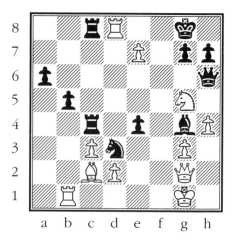

LOOKING BACK

Hundreds of years before the emergence of modern chess, a pawn could advance only one square at a time even on its first move. Games were very slow; it seemed to take forever for the two armies to actually engage on the battlefield. There came a time, before the 13th century, when some genius introduced the two-square advance possibility for a pawn's first move. This sped up the game considerably and brought the opposing forces into contact almost immediately. The two-square pawn move also allowed quicker development of the pieces.

But players found that they could use the double pawn move to bypass an advancing enemy pawn, thus avoiding capture or blocking the pawns in that area. The results were reduced pawn exchanges, limited piece activity, and stupefyingly slow and boring games.

Then, *voilà*! The en passant rule, introduced around 1500, solved the problem and helped make chess one of the most popular of all games, a status it enjoys to this day, five hundred years later and counting.

The laws of chess require a king to get out of check immediately. Black's king has no safe square (f7 is controlled by White's knight on g5), so he has no choice but to capture the checking rook with Rxd8.

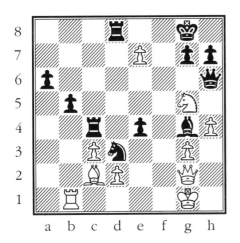

Now comes the killer final move: exd8=Q checkmate! (The equals sign means promotion.) White promotes to a queen even though his original queen is still on the board (on g2).

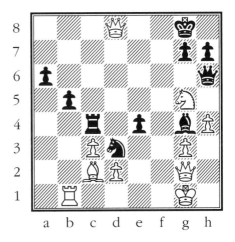

It's important to appreciate that the brave pawn that has just become a queen and ended the enemy king's life started as a common foot soldier. Respect your pawns! In the words of the great 1920s grandmaster Savielly Tartakower, "Never lose a pawn and you will never lose a game."

By the way, White could have promoted the pawn to a rook (exd8=R) instead of a queen with the same result. This is called underpromotion.

10

CHECK AND CHECKMATE

CHECK

A direct attack on the king—that is, a threat to capture it on the next move—is called check.

A king is required by the laws of chess to get out of check immediately. If it cannot, it is checkmated and the game is over.

A check is often a strong move because it limits the opponent's options or gains time. But not all checks are good moves. A check is a good move when it's part of a plan or if it gains time or material. Otherwise it can be a loss of time or a mistake that weakens your position. There's an old saying: "Patzer sees a check, patzer gives a check." A patzer, in chess jargon, is a weak, blundering player.

In casual play, many players warn their opponents by announcing "check!" but this is not required. Among strong players, who are perfectly capable of seeing for themselves when their king is in check, such warnings are considered annoying.

There are three ways to get out of check.
• Move it to a square that is not under attack.
• Capture the enemy man that's attacking it.
• Block the attack by interposing one of your own men between your king and the attacking man.

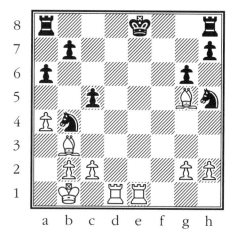

The Black king is in check. Can you find its only escape square?

THE LANGUAGE OF CHESS

The words check and mate are derived from the Old Persian words *shah*, "king," and *mat*, "defeated" or "defenseless." When Arabic-speaking countries learned chess from the Persians, they naturally translated Persian chess terms into Arabic. As it happened, the word *mat* already existed in Arabic, meaning "dead." Since the king is never actually captured, it never "dies," so the translation of the Old Persian *mat* as "dead" is technically imprecise.

The Black king's only escape square is f8. All the other squares the king can move to are controlled by White pieces.

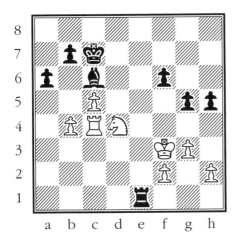

What is the only way White can get out of check?

The bishop on c6 is checking the White king, but the king has no place to go. White's only move is to capture the bishop with his knight on d4.

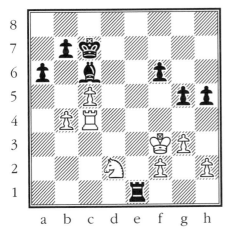

Here, White's knight is on d2 instead of d4. What are White's only two legal moves?

Since White can't capture the checking bishop or move his king, the only way he can get out of check is by interposing his knight or rook on e4.

CHECKMATE

When a king can't move out of check, capture the checking man, or cut off the check by interposing a man, the king is checkmated. Checkmate (or simply mate) ends the game at once. The king is never actually captured.

It's important to recognize the common types of checkmate positions. They will come up time and again in your games. See "Mating for Fun and Profit," page 62.

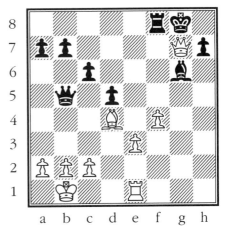

A "battery" mate. The queen and bishop on the same line form a battery.

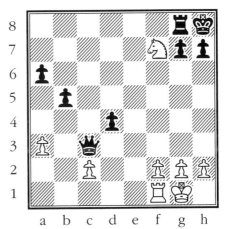

A "smothered" mate. The Black king's "air" is cut off by the edges of the board and his own rook and pawns.

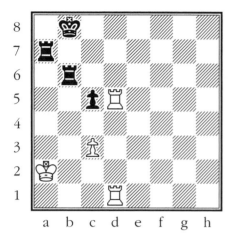

A "corridor" mate. One rook gives check while the other prevents the king's escape.

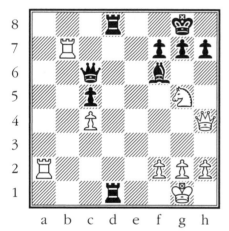

A "back rank" mate. The White king is trapped on its back rank.

The back rank mate theme is brilliantly exemplified in this famous game, played in New Orleans in 1920.

Torre

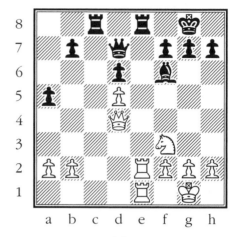

Adams

Black's rook on e8 is attacked twice, by the two White rooks, one backing up the other, and defended twice, by the rook on c8 and the queen on d7. If one of those defenders is pulled away, the captures on e8 will result in a back rank mate.

White	Black
1 Qg4!	Qb5

Black can't accept the queen offer. If 1 ... Qxg4? 2 Rxe8+ Rxe8 3 Rxe8 mate. And 1 ... Rxe2 is answered by 2 Qxd7. The same key idea is repeated in the following moves. To avoid mate, Black must maintain the defense of the rook on e8 as well as the back rank.

2 Qc4!	Qd7
3 Qc7!	Qb5
4 a4	Qxa4
5 Re4	Qb5

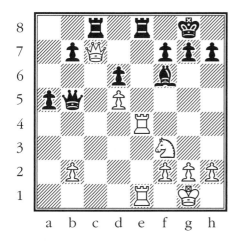

6 Qxb7!

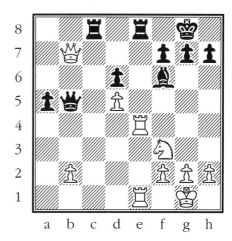

The end. Black can't take the queen or the rook on e4 because of mate on the back rank. So he must lose his queen.

11

CALLING IT A DRAW

You can't win 'em all. But not winning does-n't mean you have to lose. The gods of chess have made it possible to draw, which is nei-ther winning nor losing.

In tournaments, the winner of a game earns one point, the loser zero. A draw gives each player half a point. In casual play, the score usually doesn't matter, but still, it's bet-ter to draw than to lose, don't you think? If you find yourself in a losing position, you can congratulate yourself if you manage to get a draw and earn half a point. On the other hand, some players feel that to draw a game is to *lose* half a point.

Formal competition is governed by a dou-ble clock or timer that allows you to stop your own clock and simultaneously start your opponent's. Because of the time controls, players are bound by strict rules of behavior, especially the prohibition against annoying or distracting your opponent by making repeated draw offers.

To offer a draw in a tournament, first make your move, then whisper a draw offer, then stop your clock. Your opponent considers the offer on his turn while his clock is running. If he accepts, he makes some silent gesture of agreement or stops the clocks. If he doesn't, he simply makes his move and the game pro-ceeds. You can't offer a draw again unless and until your opponent has himself offered a draw and you have declined it. Such is the psychological warfare that takes place about two feet above the board.

There are several ways to draw a game.
• agreement between the players
• stalemate
• threefold repetition of the same position (which includes perpetual check)
• insufficient mating material
• the 50-move rule

DRAW BY AGREEMENT

Very often a position arises in which neither player has an advantage and there is no pawn majority on either side of the board. A pawn majority could eventually yield a passed pawn and some hope of making progress, but without that possibility this kind of "bal-anced" position offers virtually no winning chances unless somebody falls asleep.

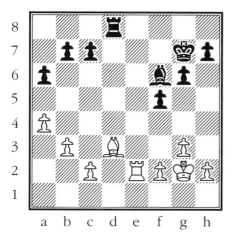

Black to move. A balanced position with no winning chances for either side.

Sometimes a player has one kind of advantage—an extra pawn, for instance—and the opponent has a compensating advantage of another kind, such as better pawn structure, more effective pieces, or a strong attack. Or there may be pawn majorities on both sides, with the possibility of a passed pawn for each player. In these kinds of positions the two sides have equal winning chances—and equal losing chances. Trying to win such positions is to risk losing. Risks are part of chess, of course, but it's often prudent to accept a draw rather than take *foolhardy* risks. Losing half a point is better than losing a whole point.

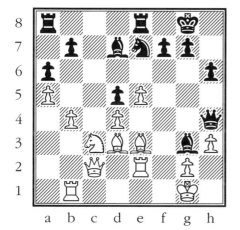

Black to move. In this unbalanced position, White has a powerful center but Black has attacking chances.

STALEMATE

When you have no legal move and your king is *not* in check, you are stalemated. As illogical as it seems, this is a draw. If you have no legal move and your king *is* in check, you are checkmated and you lose.

It's very easy to fall into a stalemate trap just when you think you're winning.

White to move.

White has a winning position because his passed pawn can't be stopped from becoming a queen. But advancing the pawn immediately would be a gross blunder because of stalemate. The correct method is to force the Black king out of the corner to avoid stalemate: 1 Kg6 Kg8 2 Kh6 Kh8 3 g6 (no stalemate this time: the Black king has a legal move) 3 ... Kg8 4 g7 Kf7 5 Kh7, and the pawn queens on the next move. Study this basic endgame position carefully until you're sure you understand how it works.

CHANGE THE RULES?

Many chess fans, whether they play the game or watch others play, dislike draws. They prefer a decisive conclusion with a winner and a loser. Although draws are an established feature of chess, players throughout history have tried to find ways to eliminate them or reduce their number. None has gained a significant following so far.

One idea, based on a rule similar to that used in the Japanese game shogi, a cousin of chess, would make it illegal to repeat a position. Another suggestion, the most logical one I've seen, is to count stalemate not as a draw but as a win for the stalemating player and a loss for the opponent. (A few centuries ago, one theorist considered stalemates dishonorable and wanted them to count as a loss for the *stalemating* player!) This old idea has many adherents, but general acceptance, if it comes at all, will take at least a few generations. It would radically change the endgame and the middlegame and would affect even some opening variations. Changes of such magnitude do not happen every day in chess. The last ones occurred 500 years ago.

Another classic stalemate pitfall:

White to move.

Of course White will promote his pawn. But the hasty c7-c8=Q is stalemate! This is one of those times when the queen is just too strong. The right move is *under*promotion with c7-c8=R! Black must now move his king to a6, and White will play Ra8 mate.

This famous stalemating combination is from a game played at the London 1883 tournament. Set up the position on your chessboard and enjoy this delightful finish.

Better yet, try to play through the moves in your mind, *without* setting up the pieces.

Englisch

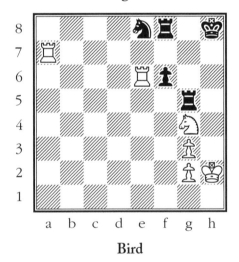

Bird

White to move.

White sees a tricky way to win Black's f-pawn. The pawn is defended by Black's knight on e8, so White sacrifices a valuable rook to get rid of the knight, expecting to win Black's rook a couple of moves later and also collect the f6 pawn.

1 Rxe8

He hopes Black will play 1 ... Rxe8 when White's 2 Nxf6 has two threats: to take Black's rook on e8 and to deliver checkmate on h7 with the rook, winning in either case.

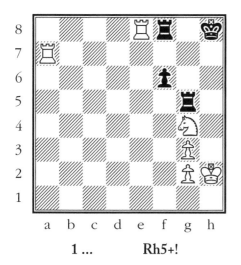

1 ...   Rh5+!

Oops. Black foils White's plan, though White may not realize it yet.

2 Kg1   Rxe8

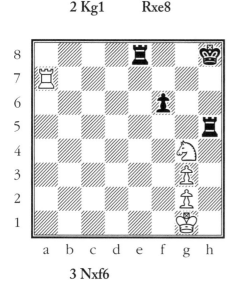

3 Nxf6

The point of White's little combination. He has won the pawn and is attacking both Black rooks. But now Mr. Bird gets the bird. Have you noticed that Black's king has no legal move? Why is that significant?

3 ...   Rh1+!
4 Kxh1

White has only a choice of evils. If 4 Kf2 Rf1+! 5 Kxf1 Re1+! 6 Kxe1 stalemate. If 6 Kf2 Rf1+ and Black can check perpetually because if White ever takes the rook, it's stalemate.

4 ...   Re1+

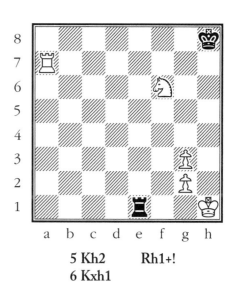

5 Kh2   Rh1+!
6 Kxh1

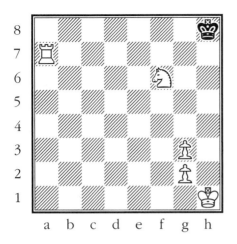

Stalemate!

One of the most widely published stalemate combinations of modern times took place in the U.S. Championship of 1962–63. The legendary grandmaster Sammy Reshevsky was playing Black against grandmaster Larry Evans. Despite mistakes by both sides, Reshevsky gradually outplayed his opponent and finally reached this position. He has just played 48 ... Qxg3, threatening five different mates (Re1, Rh2, Qe1, Qh2, Qg2). What is White to do?

Reshevsky

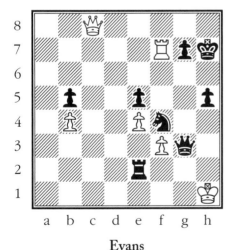

Evans

49 Qg8+!!

This has been called the "Stalemate of the Century," and it's truly a heart-stopping

moment. It's impossible to exaggerate the elation Evans must have felt when he thought of this move. And try to imagine how poor Sammy must have felt.

| 49 ... | Kxg8 |

There's no choice. If 49 ... Kg6 or 49 Kh6 50 Qxg7 mate.

50 Rxg7+!

The final blow. Black agreed to a draw, since 50 Kxg7 or 50 Qxg7 is stalemate.

THREEFOLD REPETITION BY PERPETUAL CHECK

This type of draw results from a series of consecutive checks by the same player, forcing the opponent to repeat the same position perpetually. It's a type of threefold repetition of the same position, which is a draw (see below). Here's a classic example from tournament play.

Botvinnik

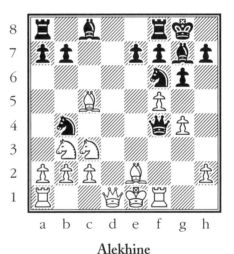

Alekhine

Black to move.

This is the conclusion of a famous game between two chess giants, Alexander Alekhine (White) and Mikhail Botvinnik, played at the great Nottingham tournament in 1936. Alekhine, world champion from

1927 to 1935 and again from 1937 until his death in 1946, was the most feared player of the age. Botvinnik was an up-and-coming young rival who was to become world champion after Alekhine's death. This game, their first meeting, had been highly anticipated, and its surprising finish created a sensation.

Alekhine delayed castling in order to get an early attack going, and indeed Black seemed to be in trouble. In the position on the previous page, White is simultaneously attacking Black's queen (with the rook on f1) and knight (with the bishop on c5). Black must move his queen, but where? There is no place where it can save itself and also protect the knight. It looks like Black is going to lose a piece.

But Botvinnik has foreseen this position and now sacrifices not one but two pieces to take advantage of the White king's unsafe position.

1 ...   Qxh2!

Leaving the knight on b4 unprotected.

2 Bxb4

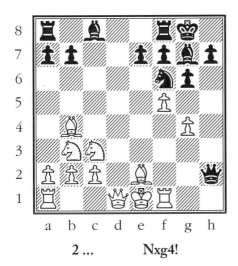

2 ...   Nxg4!

Sacrificing a second piece to set up perpetual check.

3 Bxg4

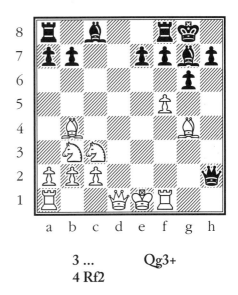

3 ...   Qg3+
4 Rf2

Blocking the check. The alternative is not acceptable. If 4 Ke2, Black takes the bishop on g4 with check and then takes White's other bishop, ending up with extra material as well as a winning positional advantage. If 4 Kd2, Black wins crushingly with 4 ... Bh6+.

4 ...   Qg1+

Nothing else does the job. For instance, 4 ... Qe3+ allows White to escape the perpetual check and keep his extra piece with 5 Qe2. Here we see the point of Black's knight sacrifice on g4: the bishop can't interpose on f1.

5 Rf1   Qg3+
6 Rf2

And so on, forever. Neither side can afford to vary, and so the game ends without a winner. But many believed that Botvinnik was the moral victor, not only for achieving a draw in his first encounter with the great Alekhine, but also for doing it so brilliantly.

The following position, a 1927 study by Weenink, was shown to me by Bruce Pandolfini, the renowned New York chess pedagogue, founder of New York City's pioneer Chess-in-the-Schools program, and author of more than thirty books.

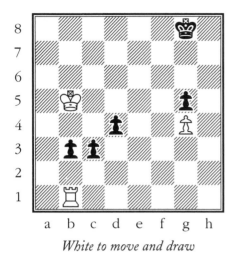

White to move and draw

What is White to do? How can he possibly stop those pawns, at least one of which must make it to queenhood? A plausible try is 1 Rxb3, but then 1 ... c2 brings down the curtain. The surprising solution is—damn the torpedoes, full speed ahead!—1 Kc6!! c2 2 Re1! b2 3 Re8+ Kf7 4 Kd7, with perpetual check at e6, e7, and e8 no matter what Black does. Neat, eh?

After 4 Kd7

THREEFOLD REPETITION

The rule states that a game is a draw when the same position occurs (or is about to occur) for the third time with the same player to move each time. The situation is similar to perpetual check but with two differ-

ences. First, checks are not a necessary component. Second, the position need not be repeated on consecutive moves. For example, if a position that occurs on White's 33rd move is repeated on White's 40th and 44th moves, the game is a draw by repetition.

This is a position from a game played at Marienbad in 1925.

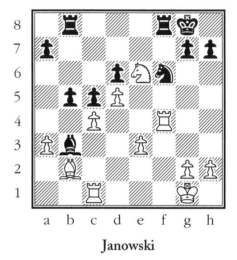

Janowski

Black to move

Black had won a pawn on the queenside and was threatening to make things worse for White by playing bxc4, removing the protector of White's important pawn on d5. So White made a counter-threat by playing Ne6 (diagram), attacking Black's rook on f8, which is protecting the knight on f6. Now Black doesn't have time to carry out his plan on the queenside. Since his rook is worth more than the knight, Black can't let it be taken. And if the rook moves off the f-file, White will play 2 Bxf6 gxf6 3 Rxf6, regaining his pawn and setting up dangerous threats.

1 ...   Rf7
2 Ng5

Attacking the rook again.

2 ...   Rf8

And again the rook can't leave the f-file.

| 3 Ne6 | Rf7 |
| 4 Ng5 | Rf8 |

Now 5 Ne6 would have repeated the position of the diagram for the third time, so the game was declared a draw.

INSUFFICIENT MATING MATERIAL

This is obviously a draw. Why? Because checkmate is impossible. One king cannot check the other, and there are no other pieces on the board.

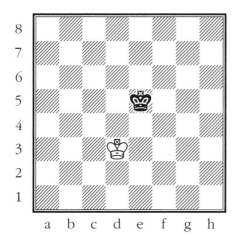

So let's give White a piece

This is a draw, too. Try as you might, you will never be able to mate the Black king.

When neither player has the minimum material necessary to force checkmate even if the opponent plays like a dunce, the game is a "theoretical" draw. With no pawns on the board, the minimum material needed to force checkmate is a rook. You can also force mate with two bishops, with a bishop and knight, or with a queen, as well as with other combined forces (but not two knights). However, a single pawn may be enough because of the possibility that it might be promoted.

But some positions with pawns can't be won, despite appearances. Here's one of them.

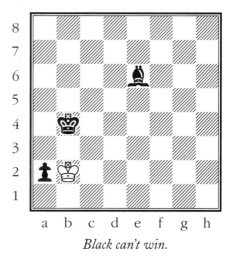

Black can't win.

Black has the great material advantage of a bishop and pawn but can't win the game because his light-square bishop can never control a1, the queening square. Black can't force White's king away from that square but can only stalemate it. White just shuttles his king between a1 and b2 and there's nothing Black can do about it. For instance, if it's White's move, he plays Ka1. If Black moves his king to a3, b3, or c3, White is stalemated. Or if Black moves his bishop along the a2-b8 diagonal, White puts his king back on b2.

THE 50-MOVE RULE

In competitive chess, a draw is declared if 50 moves are played with neither a pawn advance nor a capture. If either event occurs within that period, the count begins again. In recent years computers have discovered six rare endgame positions that can be won but require more than 50 moves. The 50-move rule was amended in 1988 to take those positions into account.

SECTION I EXERCISES

Most of these exercises are related to material covered in Section I. More exercises appear at the end of Section II and cover material in that section. To get the greatest benefit from these positions, set them up on your chessboard and try to solve them without moving the pieces or looking at the solutions. Then check the solutions on page 122.

EXERCISE 1

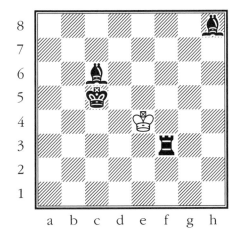

To which squares, if any, can the White king legally move?

EXERCISE 2

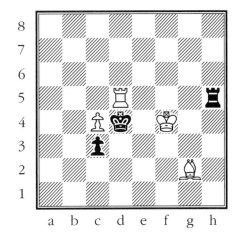

Where can the Black king move?

EXERCISE 3

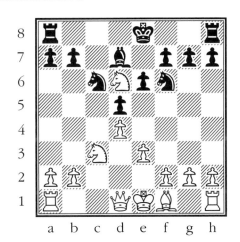

Black to move. On which side can he castle?

EXERCISE 4

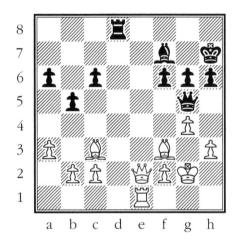

White wins a piece in two moves.

EXERCISE 5

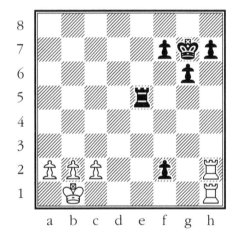

What is Black's best move?

EXERCISE 6

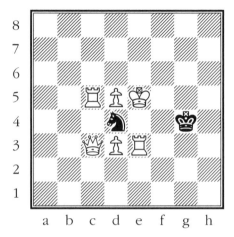

Where can the Black knight move?

EXERCISE 7

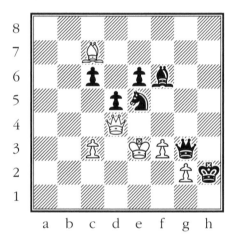

*It is Black's move. Can he move
his knight?*

EXERCISE 8

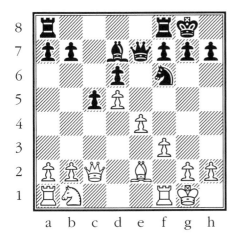

Black has just played his c-pawn from c7 to c5. How can White capture that pawn?

EXERCISE 9

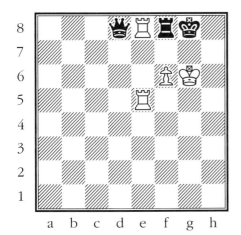

White mates in two moves by force against any defense.
(White moves, then Black, then White checkmates.)

EXERCISE 10

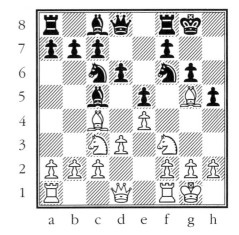

White to move wins material.

EXERCISE 11

Black wins, of course, but what's the fastest way?

=12=

MATING FOR FUN AND PROFIT

Your ultimate objective is to checkmate the enemy king. Duh. This chapter explains the so-called basic mates; i.e., situations in which, for the sake of clarity and simplicity, there are no pawns or pieces on the board other than those required for mate. The basic mating techniques are just that: techniques. You might compare them to a pianist's scales and arpeggios. Once you have them "in the fingers," as pianists say, you can apply them readily in your games.

In chess parlance, queens and rook are the "major" or "heavy" pieces, bishops and knights the "minor" or "light" pieces.

MATE WITH THE QUEEN

Since the queen is the strongest piece, this is the easiest and quickest checkmate. First let's see a checkmate position.

Now let's zip back in time to an earlier position and see how this mate came about. The position is the first that appears in Reuben Fine's *Basic Chess Endings*.

White mates in 9 moves.

Two things to remember: One, the queen, despite its great power, can't do it alone but needs the help of the king. Two, without pawns or other men on the board, you cannot mate the king in the middle but must first drive it to the edge. As you play over the following moves (given by Fine), watch how Black tries to stay near the center and avoid the edge while White brings his king toward the center and uses his queen to force the Black king away.

1 Kb2	Kd5
2 Kc3	Ke5

3 Qg6

Cutting off the top three rows from the Black king.

3 ...	Kf4
4 Kd4	Kf3
5 Qg5	

Forcing the king to the first two ranks.

5 ...	Kf2
6 Qg4	Ke1
7 Ke3	Kf1
8 Qg7	

Not 8 Qg3?? stalemate.

| 8 ... | Ke1 |
| 9 Qa1 mate | |

White could also mate with 9 Qg1.

MATE WITH TWO ROOKS

This is one of those mates you will probably never see because your opponent will have resigned long before it is reached. But you should know how it works anyway. As you will see in the next section, a single rook is really all you need; having two is like having two Rolls Royces. You can give one away and still get where you're going in style. The rooks cut off the enemy king's escape and drive it to the edge. There are many ways to do it; this is just one of them.

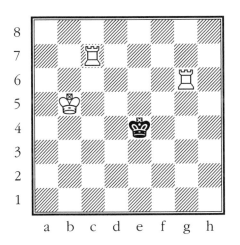

1 Rc5	Kd4
2 Rg4+	Ke3
3 Rc3+	Kd2
4 Kb4	Kd1
5 Rg2	Ke1
6 Rc1 mate	

MATE WITH ONE ROOK

This mate is a little trickier. Again, the enemy king must be driven to the edge of the board before it can be mated. We're going to try a little "retro-analysis" here. First I'll show you a position in which the Black king is mated (Diagram A); then a position a few moves earlier (Diagram B); finally, a position a few moves before that (Diagram C). Here's a typical target position in which Black has been mated.

Diagram A: Black has been mated.

Now let's back up a few moves and look at how the mating process works once the Black king has been confined.

Diagram B: White mates in 5 moves.

Diagram C: White to move and mate.

White's rook prevents the Black king from moving off the a-file.

1 Kc4

Black now has no choice but to move his king to a6. The key idea, which works on any edge of the board, is that Black can't go face to face against the White king with 1 ... Ka4 because of 2 Ra1 mate. This pattern, crucial in rook endgames, is repeated several times in the following moves.

1 ...	Ka6
2 Kc5	Ka7
3 Kc6	Ka8
4 Kc7	

And now the Black king must give up its miserable life.

4 ...	Ka7
5 Ra1 mate	

Now let's go back to an even earlier position of the same game and see how to the king is pushed against the wall.

Before playing over the following moves, remember how the queen and king maneuvered the Black king to the edge of the board. A similar technique applies here: White forces Black to move his king away from the center and toward the edge. Try it yourself, but don't worry about how long it takes; you can refine your technique with practice. For now, the important thing is to accomplish the goal. Here's one way to do it.

1 Kf4	Kd4
2 Rd1+	Kc5
3 Ke4	Kc4
4 Rc1+	Kb5
5 Kd4	Kb4
6 Rb1+	Ka5

We have now reached the position of Diagram B. The king has been pushed to the edge and will not be able to escape.

MATE WITH THE MINOR PIECES

Forget about mating with the two knights. Although you can set up a mate position with two knights, the position cannot be forced in actual play. Anyway, the situation will never occur in your games. Nor will you ever see two bishops or bishop and knight against a king with nothing else on the board. Although they are so rare as to be ignored by almost all chess manuals, they are useful exercises. Think of them as puzzles in which you have to find the shortest solution.

Here is a two-bishop position with its solution. Set up your own position and try to find the shortest mate. This exercise is quite difficult, as the Black king always seems to slither out of the net. You will need to learn how to use waiting moves that threaten nothing but merely force the enemy king to move.

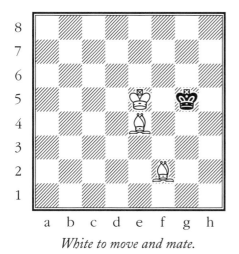

White to move and mate.

This time the king must be driven not only to an edge but also to a corner.

1 Bf5	Kh6
2 Kf6	Kh5
3 Be6	Kh6
4 Bg4	Kh7
5 Kf7	Kh6
6 Be3+	Kh7
7 Bf5+	Kh8
8 Bd4 mate	

The mate with bishop and knight against the king is so difficult that it stumps even

many grandmasters. It almost never occurs in practice, so why bother studying it? In some positions the solution could require 34 moves! Here's the final sequence of the solution given by Fine. This time the king must be driven not only to the edge and a corner but also to a corner the same color as the bishop.

You might like to play around with this position for a while and keep coming back to it as your chess improves. It's a helpful exercise in using the pieces cooperatively.

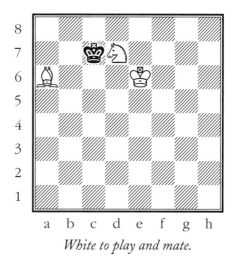

White to play and mate.

1 Bb5	Kd8
2 Nb6	Kc7
3 Nd5+	Kd8
4 Kd6	Kc8
5 Ke7	Kb7
6 Kd7	Kb8
7 Ba6	Ka7
8 Bc8	Kb8
9 Ne7	Ka7
10 Kc7	Ka8
11 Bb7+	Ka7
12 Nc6 mate	

13

CHESS FAMILY VALUES

Material—pieces and pawns—is a fundamental element of chess. As a rule, the player with a material advantage will win the game. The greater the advantage, the greater the likelihood of winning. On a real-life battlefield, the larger army is the stronger one and wins either by overwhelming the smaller army or by simple attrition: if equal numbers of units are eliminated on both sides, eventually the weaker side will be reduced to nothing. Although this is essentially true in chess too, there's an important difference: in chess all men are not created equal.

At many points in a game, often in the very beginning, you will have opportunities to trade, or exchange, pieces or pawns. When considering an exchange, you obviously need to know whether it's good for you or for your opponent.

The simplest way to know is to compare the strengths, or values, of the men involved.

The strength of a piece is measured by its mobility. The strongest pieces are those with the greatest scope. The pawn, which has the least mobility (until it gets promoted), is given a value of 1; this number is the basis for comparing the values of the other men. As determined by centuries of experience and more recently by computer analysis of millions of games, the following are the accepted relative values for the purpose of calculating exchanges.

Table of Unit Values

Pawn	1
Knight	3
Bishop	3+
Rook	5
Queen	9
King	0 (5)

Because the king can't be captured or exchanged, it has no practical exchange value; it is, you might say, priceless. Although during most of the game it has little mobility or fighting power, in the endgame it's a strong piece.

The diagram will help you compare. To convince yourself of the validity of the above unit values, count the number of squares each piece can move to. Note the increased mobility of some of the pieces when they're in or near the center.

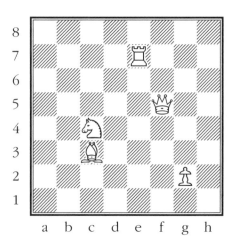

THE LANGUAGE OF CHESS

The word "exchange" has two meanings in chess. The general meaning of the verb "to exchange" is to trade one of your units for one belonging to your opponent or to make equivalent captures. The other meaning, the noun "the exchange," refers specifically to the difference in value between a rook and a bishop or knight. When you capture your opponent's rook and he gets in return your knight or bishop, you win "the exchange."

Exchanging any piece (except the queen) for the opponent's queen is usually called "winning the queen." Strictly speaking, however, in most cases the queen is not won but traded for a unit of lesser value.

In Russian and some other Eastern European languages, the difference in value between a rook and a minor piece is called "the quality."

The queen is the strongest piece because it has the greatest mobility. It can move to 25 squares when in or near the center, at least 21 squares when in or near a corner.

The rook can move to 14 squares no matter where it stands. The difference between the rook's mobility and the queen's approximates the difference expressed in the table of values.

The bishop can move to 13 squares from the center, seven from a corner. Although it has great range, a bishop is limited to the color it starts on. Depending on the pawn structure, a bishop can be "good" or "bad." A bad bishop is one whose mobility is hampered by many pawns on squares of its own color. A good bishop is one that is unimpeded by obstructions. In practice, odd as it may seem, the two bishops working together (the "bishop pair") are stronger than the sum of the two bishops individually.

A knight in or near the center can move to eight squares, but when it's on the edge it can move to only four. In a corner it can move to only two squares, which makes it even less mobile than a pawn. A well-placed knight—that is, in or near the center—is a strong piece. A badly placed knight—at the edge or in a corner—is a weak and ineffectual piece.

Here's a little jingle to keep in mind (unfortunately, the music, supposedly composed by P.D.Q. Bach while playing a Giuoco Piano, is lost):

Center knight, good knight.
Edge knight, good night!

A pawn can move to one or two squares on its first move, or to four possible squares if captures are available. After its first move it can move to or capture on three possible squares. Despite the pawn's unique power of promotion, it is given the lowest value because it can't move backward or sideways and has a very limited range.

What the table of unit values tells you is that, arithmetically speaking, trading a knight for three pawns is a fair deal, two rooks are worth slightly more than a queen, and so on. It's just simple arithmetic. On that basis alone, you should never want to exchange your rook for an opponent's pawn, for example, since a rook is worth five pawns.

But chess is not arithmetic, thank god. The table of unit values is a reliable guide to calculating exchanges *most of the time*, but there will be times when other considerations take precedence.

14

TACTICS I: Attack and Defense

"In the last analysis," writes grandmaster Reuben Fine in *The Middlegame in Chess*, "every game of chess is decided tactically." Tactics are the means by which you achieve strategic goals: gaining control of the center, occupying open files and diagonals, building direct attacks against the king, and trying to gain a material advantage. To quote Fine once again, "Theoretically, with other things equal, *any material advantage is enough to win*."

LOOKING AHEAD

We've seen (Chapter 13) how to evaluate the pieces when calculating exchanges. Now, with the help of the table of unit values (which you should have pasted on the inside of your skull), let's see how to win material and, just as important, how to avoid losing it.

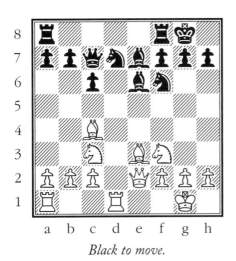

Black to move.

Black has his eye on the lovely d5 square smack-dab in the center, an ideal spot for his knight. With his pawn on c6 and his bishop on e6 both controlling that square, Black decides to move his knight there from f6.

White	Black
1 ...	Nd5

Is this a good move or a bad one? From a positional point of view, it's a peach. Tactically, though, since it loses material, it's a lemon.

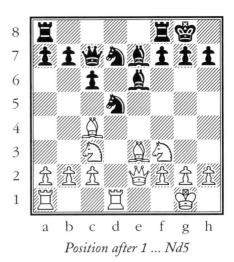

Position after 1 ... Nd5

People who don't play chess are often mystified by the ability of good players to see several moves ahead. In this case it's pretty easy: everything takes place on the same square, and all you need to do is *count*.

How many White pieces are attacking the

ON A CLEAR DAY ...

The Hungarian-Czech grandmaster Richard Réti (1889–1929) was one of the world's best players from about 1915 until his death from scarlet fever at the age of 40. In addition to his exploits at the board and his influential theoretical writings, a few of Réti's *bon mots* live on in the lore of chess.

One day an amateur player approached him with a question. "Grandmaster," asked the wide-eyed amateur, "how many moves ahead can you see?"

"Only one," Réti replied, "but it's the best one."

knight on d5? Three: the bishop on c4, the knight on c3, and the rook on d1.

How many Black men are defending it? Two: the bishop on e6 and the pawn on c6.

There are two general rules to keep in mind when considering whether or not to capture:

Rule number one: *If attackers outnumber defenders of the same or lower values, the capture wins material. If defenders outnumber attackers, the capture loses material.* See rule number two below.

Check it out (do this in your head, just as you would have to do during an actual game):

2 Nxd5	Bxd5
3 Bxd5	cxd5
4 Rxd5	

And White has won a pawn.

If you can work out this short sequence of captures and recaptures in your head, you can look ahead three moves!

MEASURE TWICE, CUT ONCE

This bit of folk wisdom can well be applied to chess. The touch-move rule (which I insist should be scrupulously observed even in casual games) means that if you touch a man you must move it, and once you move it, it stays moved. As they say, a move played is a move made. Common sense tells you, therefore, that it's very important when making exchanges or captures to be sure you've calculated correctly.

By the way, if you touch a man and decide not to move it—you're merely adjusting it on its square or you've changed your mind at the last moment—you must tell this to your opponent by whispering "*j'adoube,*" which is French for "I adjust." Players who do this frequently are considered to be deliberately distracting their opponents. In formal competition, this is a serious enough infraction to result, in extreme cases, in forfeiture.

Here comes rule number two: *When capturing or exchanging, always consider the values of the units involved.* Look at the next diagram and decide whether or not it's a good idea for White to capture the pawn on e4. The pawn is attacked three times (by knight, bishop, and rook) but defended only twice (by pawn and knight).

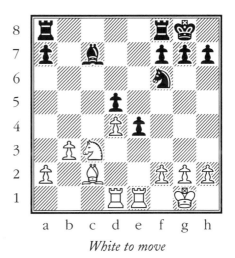

White to move

If you merely count attackers and defenders, capturing on e4 should win material, right? But see what happens after the following moves (play them in your head!):

1 Nxe4   dxe4
2 Bxe4   Nxe4
3 Rxe4

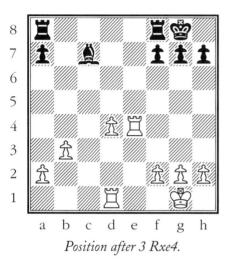

Position after 3 Rxe4.

The smoke has cleared and we can now see what's been won or lost. In the previous diagram each side had two rooks, one knight, one bishop, and six pawns. Now, after the captures and recaptures on e4, each side has two rooks, Black has one minor piece and four pawns, while White has no minor piece but six pawns. The net result: White has lost a piece in exchange for two pawns. A bad deal.

What happened here was that, although the *number* of attackers and defenders favored White, the *values* of the attackers and defenders were unequal, and this tilted the equation in Black's favor. On White's first move he took a pawn, but on Black's first move he took a *knight*.

The two rules above are general guidelines that apply in most cases. In chess, as we never tire of telling you, every rule has exceptions. It's the mark of a good player to recognize when a rule can be broken.

=15=

TACTICS II: Double Trouble

A basic tactic in chess is the double attack. When you make two threats at the same time, your opponent usually won't be able to defend against both of them and will have to make some material or positional concession. Double attacks on two enemies by a single man are called forks. We'll talk about forks in another chapter. Here we're interested in other kinds of double attacks.

The strongest double attack is one that threatens checkmate and also threatens something else. Since the mate must be prevented whatever the cost, the attacker will be free to carry out his other threat.

White wins material by means of a double threat

In this position White can threaten not only to mate Black's king but also to win his queen. With 1 Ng5 White threatens both 2 Qxh7 mate and 2 Nxe4. Black must play 1 ... h6 to avert mate (always the first priority), and White then takes the queen with 2 Nxe4.

Here's another version of the same idea but somewhat trickier. Do you see how White wins with a double threat?

White to move and win material

With 1 Nf4 White makes two threats. The obvious one is to capture Black's queen. But notice also that White's rook and Black's king are both on the h-file with only a pawn between them. This is always a potentially dangerous situation for the king. In this case, if White could get his knight to g6, giving check, the h-pawn would not be able to capture it because it's pinned; that is, it can't move off the h-file because of White's rook (we'll talk about pins in the next chapter).

Therefore the Black king would have to move out of check, and then the knight could capture the rook on e7. The moves are: 1 Nf4 Qd7 2 Ng6+ Kg8 3 Nxe7+ and White wins a rook for a knight.

So-called discovered attacks, especially discovered checks, are among the strongest tactical weapons at your disposal. Here's a rather obvious example:

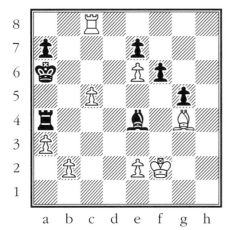

How can Black win material with a double attack?

Unprotected enemy pieces are red flags to the alert tactical player. Here White's rook on c8 and bishop on g4 are both looking for trouble, and Black gives it to them with a single blow: 1 ... Bb7!. The bishop attacks the rook and also "discovers" an attack by Black's rook on the White bishop. White's can't protect both pieces and must lose one of them.

Here's another example of a discovered attack, stripped to its essentials:

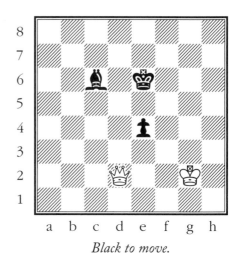

Black to move.

By playing 1 ... e3+!, Black attacks White's queen with the pawn and also "discovers" check by his bishop against the White king. White is forced to move his king, allowing Black to win White's queen.

One of the most picturesque mating patterns, a "smothered" mate, involves a discovered check.

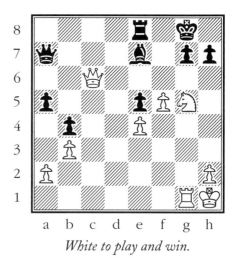

White to play and win.

White	Black
1 Qc4+	Kh8
2 Nf7+	Kg8

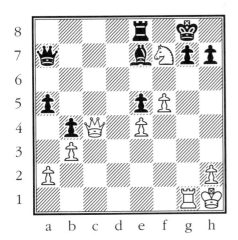

It's beautiful to see White's queen lined up with Black's king. Wherever the knight moves, it discovers check by the White queen. Where should it move?

3 Nh6+!

White could play 3 Nxe5+, but why bother taking a pawn when mate is in the offing? Black can't take the knight, of course, because his g-pawn is pinned.

3 ...   Kh8

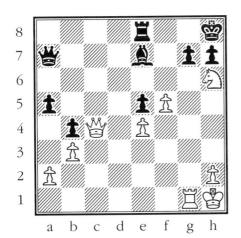

One of America's top players in the 1940s through the 1960s was I.A. Horowitz, fondly called Al by everybody. Al was the co-founder of *Chess Review* magazine (which later merged with *Chess Life*) and for a long time was the chess columnist for *The New*

York Times. One of his favorite words to describe a powerful move was the slang term "sockdolager." As a small homage to Al, I preserve that old-fashioned but expressive word here to describe White's next move.

4 Qg8+!

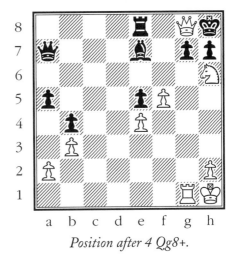

Position after 4 Qg8+.

A sockdolager if there ever was one. Black can't take the intruder with his king so he must take it with his rook.

4 ...   Rxg8

But then ...

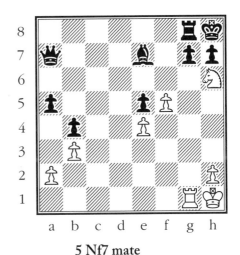

5 Nf7 mate

The classic smothered mate. The Black king is locked in an airless cell at h8.

TACTICS III: In the Kitchen

One of the oddities of chess is that some of the best tactical devices—forks, pins, and skewers—are not named for the weapons of war but for kitchen utensils.

FORK FUN

Every chessman, including the pawn, has the ability to attack at least two enemy men at the same time; kings and knights can attack three or more enemies at once. A multiple attack by a single man is a fork. There are all sorts of forks: pawn forks, knight forks, bishop forks, rook forks, and king forks—everything but the sterling silver forks you got as a wedding gift, now tarnishing in the credenza. Here are a few of the most common types.

The pawn fork: the pawn attacks both knight and bishop.

An elementary pawn fork can strike like lightning in the opening when one side is negligent about where he puts his minor pieces. Observe:

White	Black
1 d4	d5
2 Nc3	e6
3 Nf3	Bd6?

The general rule in the opening is to develop knights before bishops. There's a good reason for this: the best squares for the knights in the opening are fairly obvious—f3, c3, f6, and c6, where they attack central squares—while the bishops have more choices and should wait to see which is best depending on the opponent's moves.

4 e4   Nf6?

Black attacks White's e-pawn a second time, but this move is an outright blunder.

5 e5

THE LANGUAGE OF CHESS

Not long ago, a hot debate raged in the electronic pages of a Dutch chess club newsletter concerning the proper usage of the word "fork" in chess. The aggressors in the argument proposed that the chess fork, since it gets its name from the familiar dining utensil, can point with both prongs only in the same direction, like its namesake. According to this literal interpretation, only a pawn can properly fork. Double attacks by other single pieces are to be called, well, something else.

Humbug. The literalists may seem to have a point, but it's mere sophistry. Other pieces, notably the king and knight, can fork with both prongs facing approximately in the same direction. A double attack by a single piece is a fork, period. So it has always been in chess and so it shall always be.

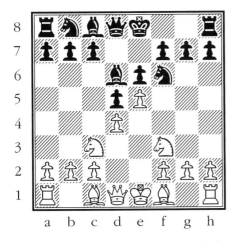

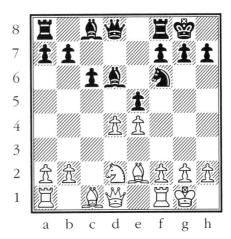

White to move and win a pawn.

The pawn forks the bishop and knight and on the next move will win one of them.

Another version of the pawn fork, the "fork trick" as it's known, sometimes seems to appear out of nowhere. It's a handy little thing to keep in your arsenal.

Everything looks so normal and peaceful, like a sunny Sunday morning. But there's trouble in the town.

1 f4!

The threat is 2 fxe5 or 2 dxe5 winning at least a pawn. If Black now plays either 1 ... exf4 or 1 ... exd4, White proceeds with the fork trick: 2 e5 wins a piece. Black should probably swallow his dignity and play 1 ... Bc7 2 fxe5, leaving White a pawn to the good and with a promising kingside attack.

Knight forks are the most treacherous.

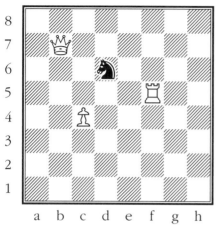

*Black's knight forks the White pawn,
rook, and queen*

Because of the knight's eccentric movement, knight forks can be hard to foresee. In this position, for example, with White to move, where will the deadly knight fork come from? Which Black pieces will be forked?

White to move.

White "puts the question" to the bishop: will it take the knight or retreat?

1 h3   Bh5?

Black doesn't see what's coming. (Do you?) He should play 1 ... Bxf3.

In many similar situations it's a good idea

to retreat the bishop and keep the pressure on the pinned knight. If White then "breaks" the pin by playing 2 g4, he seriously weakens the pawn protection of his king.

2 g4!

In this case White has a very good reason to make this weakening move, as you will soon see. Now the bishop must retreat again, since 2 ... Nxg4 3 hxg4 Bxg4 gives up a piece for only two pawns.

2 ...   Bg6

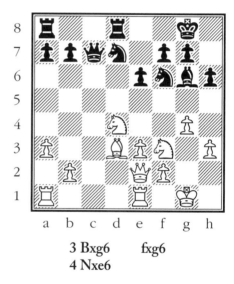

3 Bxg6   fxg6
4 Nxe6

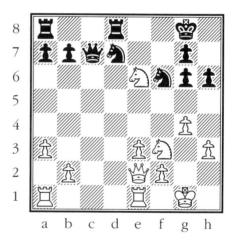

The fork. After Black's queen moves White takes the rook on d8, winning the exchange in addition to the pawn he has already won. His weakened kingside is not a problem since Black's kingside pawns have also been weakened.

PINS AND WINS

The pin, chess players like to say, is mightier than the sword. The following examples will show you why.

All pins work pretty much alike: they prevent a man from moving by pinning it to the man behind it on the same line.

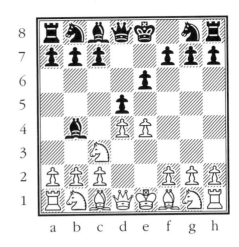

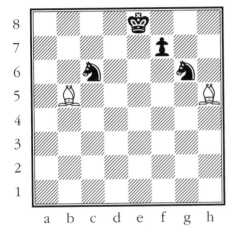

The pin of a man against its king, like the one of the left of the diagram, is sometimes called "absolute" because the pinned man cannot legally move. The situation on the right side of the board, however, is not a pin at all because a pawn stands between the knight and the king.

Here are the first few moves of a popular opening, the French Defense.

1 e4	e6
2 d4	d5
3 Nc3	Bb4

The pin. Pinning a man against its king is the strongest kind of pin. The pinned man is powerless to act while the pin is in effect. Because White's knight on c3 can't move, it is not defending the e-pawn and Black threatens to take it. The threat is easily met by 4 e5 or 4 exd5, but the point is that the pin forces White to relieve the tension in the center. With the pressure off, Black can maneuver more comfortably.

One advantage of a pin is the possibility of capturing the pinned man before it gets away. Black gets that chance if White plays 4 a3 immediately (to "kick" the bishop). Black can then play 4 ... Bxc3+, and after 5 bxc3 White's pawns on the queenside are doubled and weak.

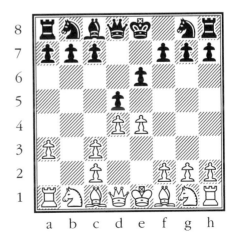

Taking the knight on c3 may or may not be the best move, but it defines both players' strategies for the next phase of the game. Black can temporarily win a pawn with 5 ... dxe4 but won't be able to keep it after 6 Qg4. More to the point is that White's pawn structure on the queenside is damaged.

Pinning a man against its queen (a "relative" pin) is also very strong but has one drawback: the pinned man may legally, and surprisingly, move. In this position, White saw an opportunity to win material by pinning the Black rook against its queen with his bishop. It sure looks like a strong move. There's just one itty-bitty problem.

ing of winning a piece by pushing it to e5, since the knight is pinned and, White assumes, can't safely move.

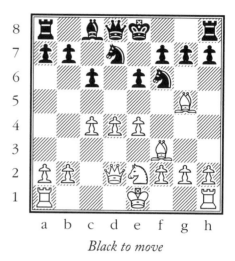

Black to move

1 ...   Nxe4!

White must now "win" the queen with 2 Bxd8, but after 2 ... Nxd2 it's clear that White has lost a pawn.

THE OPPOSITE OF A PIN

The skewer is, you might say, a reverse pin. A pin attacks a man that's shielding a more valuable man behind it on the same line; if the shield moves away, the man behind it is exposed to capture. A skewer works in much the same way, except that the skewered man is usually more valuable than the man it's shielding. The following diagrams will make this clear.

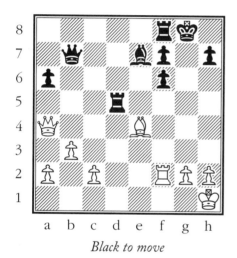

Black to move

1 ...   Rd1+!

White mates next.

Here's another example of a phantom pin. White has just played his pawn to e4, dream-

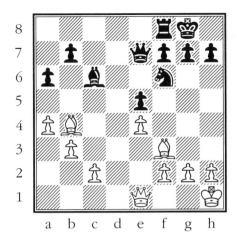 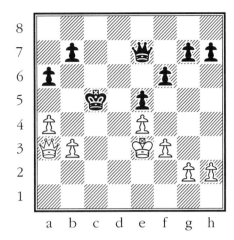

White bishop on b4 skewers the Black queen against the rook. The queen will move, of course, and White then takes the rook.

White's queen skewers the Black king and queen. The king must move and White chops the Black queen.

Opportunities for forks, pins, and skewers abound in every stage of a chess game. Be on the lookout for every chance and be alert to your opponent's opportunities!

=17=

FIRST MOVES AND THE CENTER

The object of the game, of course, is to checkmate the enemy king—but checkmate should be far from your thoughts at the beginning. In the opening, your main jobs are to occupy center squares with your pawns and develop your pieces by moving them off their starting positions.

When the game begins, your pieces are blocked by your pawns on the second rank. So first you need to advance a couple of those pawns to free your pieces—which, no less important, also begins your occupation of the center.

White's first move, for instance, might be 1 e4, a very strong move that occupies the center square e4 and, for now, attacks f5 and d5. It also opens lines for your queen and king bishop. If unchallenged, White will likely play 2 d4 and develop his knights to f3 and c3 to support his central pawns. This would give him a monopoly in the center and a tremendous advantage for the coming middlegame. Black obviously can't sit still while all this is going on. He will play a similarly strong first move like 1 ... e5, 1 ... c5, 1 ... c6, 1 ... e6, or 1 ... Nf6, and will continue by developing his pieces to claim his share of the center and keep pace with White's rapid development.

KNIGHTS BEFORE BISHOPS

When you begin to mobilize your army, develop knights before bishops. There's a good reason for this: knights are almost always developed to f3 and c3 (f6 and c6 or d7 for Black), whereas the best square for the king bishop has yet to be determined. You might want to play it to b5 (the Ruy Lopez) or c4 (the Giuoco Piano and other openings) or in some cases e2. Or you might want to develop it to g2 after playing g2-g3. Similarly for Black; the bishops have several choices but the knights' best squares are usually f6 and c6 (or d7).

PLAY ECONOMICALLY

Avoid moving the same piece twice in the opening. This is simple logic, since moving an already developed piece steals the time needed to move a piece that is not yet developed. Sometimes you can't avoid moving an already developed piece, as in the main line of the Ruy Lopez: 1 e4 e5 2 Nf3 Nc6 3 Bb5 a6, and now the bishop must either retreat or capture the knight. And then there's the provocative Alekhine's Defense: 1 e4 Nf6 2 e5 Nd5 3 d4 d6 4 c4 Nb6, where Black lures White pawns forward so they may be attacked later.

THE CENTER

Primarily, the center is the group of squares made up of e4, e5, d4, and d5. More broadly, the center also includes the twelve "secondary" squares that surround those four.

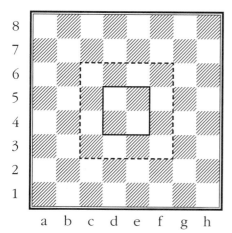

The solid lines define the primary center squares; the dashed lines define the secondary center squares surrounding the center.

You have three main objectives in the opening:

1. Establish control of at least some squares in the center by advancing your center pawns and supporting them with your pieces.

2. Develop (mobilize) all your pieces rapidly toward the center, knights before bishops.

3. Castle early to get your king away from possible danger.

If you achieve all three objectives without undue difficulty, you will have a very strong opening position with your pieces ready for action in the middlegame. In the diagram above right, both sides have almost completely developed their pieces (Black's bishop on c8 is still undeveloped, keeping his queen rook out of the game for the moment), and both kings are safely castled.

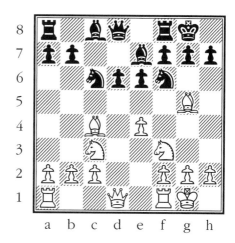

WHAT'S THE BEST MOVE?

Excellent question. Unfortunately, there is no single good answer, because there are so many choices and because your moves largely depend on what your opponent does. But there is a best strategy to follow in the opening: *play for the center*. If you nail down a fair share of center control in the first few moves, you're well on your way to a good middlegame. Remember: your main task in the opening is to reach a playable middlegame.

Here are the most common first moves for both sides. (For more detail, see Chapter 18.)

• **1 e4** occupies the central square e4 and controls f5 and d5. The pawn on e4 will be supported by a knight on c3, a rook at e1 (after castling), and the d-pawn or the f-pawn. Black's most principled responses to 1 e4 are **1 ... e5, 1 ... c5, 1 ... e6** (followed by 2 ... d5), and **1 ... c6** (followed by 2 ... d5). Each of these moves either prevents White from dominating the center or stakes Black's own claim to central space.

• **1 d4** occupies d4 and controls e5 and c5. A very important difference between 1 e4 and 1 d4 is that the pawn on d4 is already protected (by the queen on d1), whereas after 1 e4 the e-pawn will soon require defense. In response to 1 d4, Black has a variety of good moves, mainly **1 ... d5** and **1 ... Nf6**. Again, each of these moves challenges White's occupation of the center.

• **1 c4** occupies c4 and controls d5. This pawn is less influential in the center than a pawn on d4 or e4, but it is also less vulnerable. Good Black answers include **1 ... Nf6**, **1 ... c5**, and **1 ... e5**.

• **1 Nf3** controls d4 and e5. White will advance his central pawns after he castles and develops more pieces. He may also fianchetto his bishop by playing g3 and Bg2. Black can respond strongly with **1 ... Nf6** or **1 ... d5**.

• **1 g3** followed by Bg2 controls e4 and d5 and prepares castling immediately without worrying about defending central pawns. Although the flank development of a bishop (a "fianchetto") is often effective, the move g2-g3 slightly weakens the pawn structure on the kingside. And if the bishop is ever lost or traded, the dark squares around the king will be vulnerable.

Opening moves that ignore one or more of the stated principles are inferior. Beginners' moves like 1 h4 and 1 a4 violate *all three* principles.

I recommend opening the game with 1 e4, and when playing Black I recommend replying to 1 e4 with either 1 ... e5 or 1 ... c5 (Sicilian Defense). These are among the oldest and most deeply analyzed openings. Although they can get pretty complicated, the principles they're based on are clear and understandable. As you gain experience, you may prefer openings that start with 1 d4, 1 c4, 1 Nf3, or even 1 g3. As Black, you may find that after 1 e4 you prefer the so-called semi-open games with 1 ... e6 (French Defense) or 1 ... c6 (Caro-Kann Defense), and after 1 d4 you may like the Indian defenses (... g6 and ... Bg7). Reuben Fine's book *The Ideas Behind the Chess Openings* is a valuable guide for understanding opening principles.

THE IDEAL OPENING

Ideally, in the opening you want your two center pawns standing side by side on the fourth rank, protected by your knights:

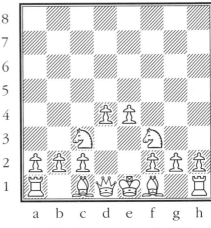

An ideal pawn center for White.

White completely controls the primary central squares as well as most of the secondary ones. But what about the opponent? It's an unfortunate fact of life that no matter which side you're playing, your opponent will not simply let you do whatever you want. In practice, you are more likely to see positions where each side controls part of the center. Here's a position after seven moves of the King's Indian Attack. White's center is not so commanding this time, and Black has excellent potential.

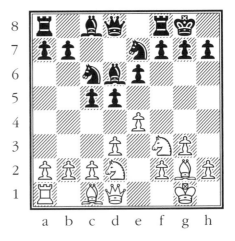

Next, a position from the King's Indian Defense (1 d4 Nf6 2 c4 g6 3 Nc3 Bg7 4 e4 d6).

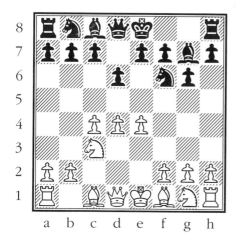

With his three pawns in the center, White seems to have an overwhelming space advantage. But the "hypermodern revolution" of the 1920s showed that White's center is not all that strong, because it can be effectively challenged. Here Black has several powerful moves just itching to be played against the White center; in particular ... e5 and ... c5. These moves strike at the d4-square, which also happens to be under the watchful eye of Black's bishop on g7. In the battle for the center, the d4-square will be one of the critical points of contention.

FIGHTING FOR THE CENTER

The myriad possibilities involving the fight for the center are well illustrated by the first few moves of one of the oldest openings in chess, the Ruy Lopez, sometimes known as the "Spanish torture."

White	*Black*
1 e4	e5

Each side stakes a claim to central space. Good alternatives for Black, each taking a different approach to the fight for the center, are 1 ... c5 (Sicilian Defense), 1 ... e6 2 d4 d5 (French Defense), and 1 ... c6 2 d4 d5 (Caro-Kann Defense). Also playable, but more provocative and difficult, are 1 ... Nf6 (Alekhine's Defense) and 1 ... g6 2 d4 d6 (Robatsch or Modern Defense).

2 Nf3

White threatens to take Black's e-pawn.

2 ...	Nc6

This is the usual move, which simply protects the pawn while developing a new piece. There could hardly be a better move, though there are a few worse ones, including 2 ... d6 (Philidor's Defense) and 2 ... f6 (Damiano's Defense). The move 2 ... Bd6?, which is so

THE LANGUAGE OF CHESS

There's a whole family of openings for both White and Black that bear the name "Indian." The name refers to an opening system that was supposedly played in India a few centuries ago. The opening was characterized by the first move Nf3 for White or Nf6 for Black, usually followed by the fianchetto of one or both bishops. It was brought to England by a master from India in the early 19th century, whose surprising successes with it caught the attention of the top players in Britain. The best-known Indian defenses are the King's Indian (1 d4 Nf6 2 c4 g6 3 Nc3 Bg7), the Queen's Indian (2 ... b6 and 3 ... Bb7), and the Nimzo-Indian (1 d4 Nf6 2 c4 e6 3 Nc3 Bb4). Since the Nimzo-Indian begins with 1 ... Nf6, it's grouped with the true Indian Defenses that feature ... g6 and ... Bg7. However, after 3 Nc3 the opening is marked by 3 ... Bb4, an invention of the great Latvian theorist Aron Nimzovich.

bad it doesn't even have a name, blocks the d-pawn and completely stifles Black's game. And don't even *think* about 2 ... Qe7.

The interesting 2 ... Nf6 (the Petroff Defense) doesn't protect the e-pawn; instead, by counterattacking White's e-pawn it leads to an immediate crisis in the center.

3 Bb5

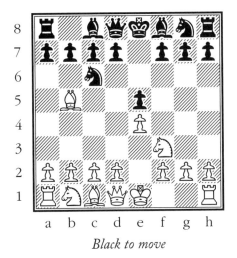

Black to move

The development of the bishop to b5 is the signature move of the Ruy Lopez. The move quite logically continues White's plan: it attacks the defender of the crucial e-pawn, threatening 4 Bxc6 followed by 5 Nxe5. Although Black can meet this threat simply and safely with 3 ... d6 (the Old Steinitz Defense) or 3 ... Bc5 (the Classical Defense), among other moves, he can afford to ignore the threat altogether.

3 ...   a6

Daring White to carry out his threat and setting a little trap. After 4 Bxc6 dxc6 5 Nxe5, Black responds with either 5 ... Qd4, attacking both the knight and the e-pawn, or 5 ... Qg5, attacking the knight and the g-pawn. In either case, Black wins back the pawn with advantage.

As a matter of fact, White *can* play 4 Bxc6 (the Exchange Variation). But the idea is not to win Black's e-pawn but to damage Black's queenside pawn structure, saddling him with a disadvantage in the endgame: 4 ... dxc6 5 d4 exd4 6 Qxd4 Qxd4 7 Nxd4. Theoretically, this leads to a favorable endgame for White. But the endgame is a long way off. As a wise man said: "Before the endgame the gods have placed the middlegame."

4 Ba4

Preserving the threat to the e-pawn and waiting to see what Black will do next. Among Black's sound choices are 4 ... b5, 4 ... d6, and 4 ... Nf6, each leading eventually to a game with equal chances.

In this opening, as in virtually all openings, White usually starts with a slight edge by virtue of the fact that he has the first move. This means he is the first to play a pawn to the center, the first to develop his pieces, the first to safeguard his king, the first to make threats. In other words, unless White plays indifferently he is the first to achieve the three principle goals of the opening. In practical terms, this gives White the "initiative." Black must take steps to avoid getting into serious trouble.

DANGER TO THE F-PAWN

In the opening position, every pawn is protected by at least one piece except the f-pawn. Because that pawn is protected only by the king, it's a tempting target for early attacks. Should the pawn be captured, the king, forced to recapture, would find itself out in the open and subject to mating attacks.

One of the most dangerous attacks comes up in the perfectly innocent-looking Two Knights Defense.

White	Black
1 e4	e5
2 Nf3	Nc6
3 Bc4	Nf6
4 Ng5	

In theory, it's not good to move the same

piece twice in the opening. But Black will have to sweat a little to prove that theory correct. What should Black do to meet the threat to his f-pawn? 4 ... Qe7 is no good because 5 Bxf7+ wins the pawn anyway.

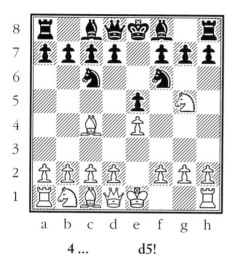

4 ...   d5!

The only reasonable move.

5 exd5

Now what? The straightforward 5 ... Nxd5 jumps headlong into the brier patch. I can't even begin to explain the bewildering complications that follow 6 Nxf7 (attacking queen and rook, thus forcing the reply) 6 ... Kxf7 7 Qf3+ (threatening to win the knight on d5) 7 ... Ke6. Believe me, it's no fun to play Black in this variation, even with a piece up. Entire books have been written about it. Take my advice and avoid the whole messy affair with 5 ... Na5.

See what I mean about the sensitivity of the f-pawn? Your best course, whether you're playing White or Black, is to develop your pieces quickly, especially the kingside pieces, and castle early.

THE LANGUAGE OF CHESS

The names ·of openings and their branching variations are not only handy shortcuts for remembering and identifying them but are also historical artifacts that memorialize the great names and places in chess all the way back to the 16th century. Most openings bear the name of a player, place, or tournament that was significant in the opening's discovery or development. Sometimes, as for example the Bishop's Opening or the Two Knights Defense, the name is simply a characteristic of the play.

One colorful example is the Poisoned Pawn Variation of the Najdorf Variation of the Sicilian Defense. The Sicilian was first analyzed, in 1617, by Carrera, who was, of course, Sicilian. One of its most popular variations, the Najdorf (pronounced NY-dorf), was played and popularized by the Polish-Argentine grandmaster Miguel Najdorf in the 1940s and later. In one branch of the Najdorf, White offers the sacrifice of his b-pawn, an offer Black would be wise to refuse; accepting it subjects Black to a powerful attack. This branch of the Najdorf tree has become known as the Poisoned Pawn Variation. Largely thanks to this particular trap, chess players are often sarcastically advised, "Never take the b-pawn, even if it's good."

Another example: the Ruy Lopez (sometimes called the Spanish Opening or Spanish Game), named for the 16th-century Spanish cleric López de Segura. One of its major branches is the Modern Steinitz Defense. This is a renovated form of the Old Steinitz Defense, which was named for Wilhelm Steinitz, the first official world champion, who promulgated this system. An offshoot of this line is the Siesta Variation, which was popularized by another world champion, José Raúl Capablanca, who played it successfully at a tournament held at the Siesta Sanatorium in Budapest in 1928.

Then there's the Two Knights Defense, so called because Black develops both knights at the start (1 e4 e5 2 Nf3 Nc6 3 Bc4 Nf6) instead of playing the Guioco Piano by developing his bishop on the third move (3 ... Bc5). In the Two Knights Defense we find a wild attacking variation with the weird name Fried Liver Attack or Fegatello Attack. Nobody seems to know how this name originated, and its meaning is often misunderstood. The Italian word *fegato* literally means liver (*fegatello* is a diminutive) but its figurative meaning is "guts" or "nerve." That pretty well describes what you need if you're going to play this variation. How the adjective "fried" got attached to it is one of those chess mysteries that may never be solved. I suspect it was intended as a joke, added by an American chess editor in the 1930s.

=18=
RECOMMENDED OPENING MOVES

This chapter contains somewhat more advanced material than the previous chapters. It'll be here when you need it.

The chart gives the recommended starting moves for both White and Black and the reasons they're recommended, which should be obvious by now. A move that develops a new piece, contributes to central control, or promotes king safety (castling) is a good move. Other moves are either time-wasting or weakening. The explanatory notes give the most common continuations.

White's 1st move	If Black plays	White should play	Because
1 e4	1 ... e5	2 Nf3 (see note 1)	Attacks Black's e-pawn and central squares, develops a new piece, prepares to castle
1 e4	1 ... c5 (2)	2 Nf3	Develops a new piece, prepares to play d4, prepares to castle
1 e4	1 ... e6 (3)	2 d4	Occupies the center, opens lines for bishops and queen
1 e4	1 ... c6 (4)	2 d4	Occupies the center, opens lines for bishops and queen
1 e4	1 ... d6, 1 ... g6 (5)	2 d4	Occupies the center, opens lines for bishops and queen
1 e4	1 ... Nf6 (6)	2 e5 Nd5 3 d4	Gains space, opens lines for bishops and queen
1 d4	1 ... d5	2 c4 (7)	Builds a strong center, attacks d5, gains space
1 d4	1 ... Nf6 (8)	2 c4	Builds a strong center, gains space
1 d4	1 ... f5 (9)	2 g3	White prepares to dominate d5 and the light squares
1 c4	1 ... e5 (10)	2 Nc3	Begins assault on d5

(1) Depending on Black's second move, this can lead to various openings. After 2 ... Nc6 White can play 3 Bb5, the characteristic move of the **Ruy Lopez**. White seems to be threatening to take Black's knight, which would leave Black's e-pawn unprotected. Suppose Black plays 3 ... a6, ignoring the threat and asking White what he intends to do with his attacked bishop. If White then carries out his threat with 4 Bxc6 dxc6 5 Nxe5, Black wins back his pawn with either 5 ... Qd4 or 5 ... Qg5.

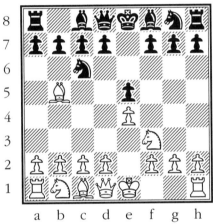

The characteristic position of the Ruy Lopez after 3 Bb5

Although 3 ... a6 is the most popular third move for Black in the Ruy Lopez, there are other good moves, among them 3 ... Bc5 (the Classical Defense), 3 ... Nf6 (the Berlin Defense), and 3 ... d6 (the Old Steinitz Defense).

Instead of 3 Bb5, White can play 3 Bc4, leading either to the Giuoco Piano after 3 ... Bc5 or to the Two Knights Defense after 3 ... Nf6.

The Italian term **Giuoco Piano** means "quiet game," but historically this opening has produced many exciting attacking games. The main line is 1 e4 e5 2 Nf3 Nc6 3 Bc4 Bc5 4 c3 Nf6 5 d4 exd4 6 dxe4 Bb4+ 7 Nc3 (sacrificing a pawn for open lines and attacking chances) or 7 Bd2.

The **Two Knight Defense** can get pretty wild, especially after 3 ... Nf6 4 Ng5 (attacking the weak pawn on f7) 4 ... d5 5 exd5 Na5 (or 5 ... Nxd5 6 Nxf7, the Fried Liver Attack). Also possible in the Two Knights after 4 Ng5 is the wild and woolly Wilkes-Barre Variation, 4 ... Bc5, in which Black ignores the threat to his f-pawn in order to continue his development, come what may.

There are other old kingside openings that are very much worth investigating. Though seldom played today (their bones were picked clean a hundred years ago), they still have a lot of life in them and offer exciting tactical play.

The **Scotch Game** begins 1 e4 e5 2 Nf3 Nc6 3 d4 exd4 4 Nxd4 and now either 4 ... Bc5 or 4 ... Nf6 (not 4 ... Nxd4? 5 Qxd4 and Black will have a hard time developing his pieces) gives both sides good play and good chances.

The **Vienna Game** opens 1 e4 e5 2 Nc3, protecting the e-pawn in advance and thus enabling White to develop smoothly without having to worry about protecting it. The main line is 2 ... Nf6 3 Bc4 Nc6 or 3 ... Bb4 (3 ... Nxe4 is the so-called Frankenstein-Dracula Variation, best met by 4 Qh5 with horrific complications).

The adventurous player can have some fun with the old **Göring Gambit** (a gambit is a pawn sacrifice in the opening) and **Danish Gambit**. The Göring is 1 e4 e5 2 Nf3 Nc6 3 d4 exd4 4 c3 dxc3 5 Nxc3, where White gives up a pawn to develop rapidly and control open lines, hoping to launch a kingside attack before Black is fully developed. The Danish is 1 e4 e5 2 d4 exd4 3 c3 dxc3 4 Bc4 cxb2 5 Bxb2, a two-pawn sacrifice to obtain a terrifying position with two bishops aimed at the Black kingside (see following diagram). But 5 ... d5 6 Bxd5 Nf6 or 5 ... Bb4+ takes some of the sting out of White's attack. And, after all, Black's extra pawn will be solid gold in the endgame (if he gets that far).

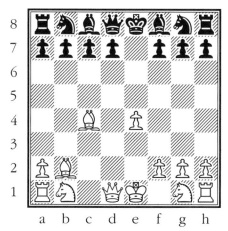

*The Danish Gambit after 1 e4 e5 2 d4
exd4 c3 3 dxc3 4 Bb4 cxb2 5 Bxb2*

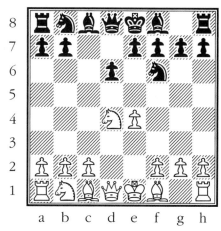

*Sicilian Defense, after 1 e4 c5 2 Nf3
d6 3 d4 cxd4 4 Nxd4 Nf6*

The **King's Gambit** starts 1 e4 e5 2 f4 exf4 3 Nf3 g5. White's purposes are to lure Black's e-pawn away from the center and, after castling, to use his rook on the half-open f-file to attack Black's kingside. Although Black has nothing to fear in this opening if he doesn't panic, he can calmly decline the gambit with 2 ... Bc5.

These old openings are rich in possibilities. As Black, of course, you have little choice once you've committed yourself with 1 ... e5, but you have nothing to worry about if you play soundly. You may get crushed at first, but the experience will do you good.

(2) This is the **Sicilian Defense**, the most popular reply to 1 e4. The Sicilian is less a defense than a counterattack. Black allows White to plant an unmolested pawn on e4 while he gains space on the queenside. After 1 e4 c5, if White is feeling frisky he can sacrifice a pawn or two for a speculative attack with 2 d4 cxd4 3 c3 (the Morra Gambit, unsound but fun). In the normal lines after 2 Nf3 d6 3 d4 cxd4 4 Nxd4 Nf6, White controls more of the center but Black will use the partly open c-file to get good counterplay with his rooks.

Black has other good second moves besides 2 ... d6, namely 2 ... e6 and 2 ... Nc6. After 2 ... Nc6 3 d4 exd4 4 Nxd4 g6, we have the Accelerated Dragon Variation, in which Black's king bishop on the long diagonal and his rooks on the c-file will give him good attacking chances.

(3) The **French Defense** is a solid, trustworthy defense for Black, despite the major problem of developing his queen bishop. After 2 d4 d5 3 e5 (the Advance Variation), it's clear that Black will have trouble with that bishop well into the middlegame. The Advance Variation gives White a space advantage on the kingside and foretells a strong attack eventually with f4, Nf3, f5, and g4, storming the Black king position. With patience, however, Black can achieve an equal game with counterplay on the queenside. In other lines, after 3 Nc3 Nf6 (the Steinitz Variation) or 3 ... Bb4 (the Winawer Variation) 4 e5 (next diagram), White will have the better chances on the kingside by using his pawns to breach the Black king's position, while Black will seek counterplay on the queenside with ... c5.

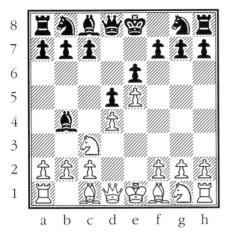

French Defense, Winawer Variation, after 1 e4 e6 2 d4 d5 3 Nc3 Bb4 4 e5

(4) The **Caro-Kann Defense** is named for the English player Horatio Caro and the Viennese master Marcus Kann, who analyzed the opening independently. It's been taken up by three world champions: Capablanca, Botvinnik, and Karpov, among many other grandmasters. The opening is known for its solidity. Black may not have much in the way of winning chances, but there's little risk of losing. In the main line, after 1 e4 c6 2 d4 d5 3 Nc3 dxe4 (best) 4 Nxe4 Bf5, Black develops all his pieces with ease, but White has a pawn in the center and great freedom of movement.

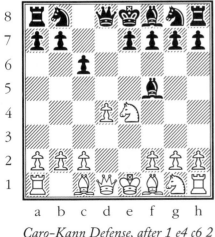

Caro-Kann Defense, after 1 e4 c6 2 d4 d5 3 Nc3 dxe4 4 Nxe4 Bf5

(5) Variously known as the **Robatsch Defense**, the **Modern Defense**, and sometimes the Pirc Defense (actually a different opening though closely related), this slippery system offers Black great flexibility but also allows White to control most of the squares in the center and develop his pieces aggressively. For example, 1 e4 d6 2 d4 Nf6 3 Nc3 g6 (diagram) followed by 4 ... Bg7, and Black will use his fianchettoed bishop to work against White's center pawns. But Black's weakened kingside will provoke a White attack in that sector.

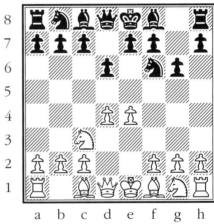

Modern Defense, after 1 e4 d6 2 d4 Nf6 3 Nc3 g6

(6) **Alekhine's Defense** is designed to lure White's pawns forward to the point where they can be attacked and weakened. The Four Pawns Attack illustrates: 1 e4 Nf6 2 e5 Nd5 3 d4 d6 4 c4 Nb6 5 f4 dxe5 6 fxe5 is a fearsomely aggressive assault but one that can be met by sober defense. The more usual approach is 1 e4 Nf6 2 e5 Nd5 3 d4 d6 4 Nf3 Bg4.

(7) For beginning players I recommend starting with 1 e4 rather than 1 d4 because the strategic goals of the kingside openings are clearer and the tactical play more instructive (and more fun). Once you've had some experience with 1 e4 (and as Black with 1 ... e5 and 1 ... c5) you'll be ready for the positional pleasures of the queenside openings.

The moves 1 d4 d5 2 c4 launch several important systems, especially the **Queen's Gambit Declined** and the **Queen's Gambit Accepted**. White is not really sacrificing his c-pawn, since he will soon get it back (but not by 3 Qa4+? Nc6 and White has to worry about his d-pawn as well as his exposed queen). One of the main lines of the Queen's Gambit Accepted (there are too many to cover adequately here) is 1 d4 d5 2 c4 dxc4 3 Nf3 Nf6 4 e3 e6 5 Bxc4 c5 6 0-0 a6 7 Qe2, where Black is not worse. The Queen's Gambit Declined is a group of openings stemming from 1 d4 d5 2 c4 e6. One of the most popular main lines is the Tartakower Variation: 3 Nc3 Nf6 4 Bg5 Be7 5 e3 0-0 6 Nf3 h6 7 Bh4 b6. Neither side dominates the center. Black will complete his development with ... Bb7 and will have equal chances in the middlegame.

(8) 1 ... Nf6 is a very flexible move that can lead to the **King's Indian Defense** (2 c4 g6), the **Queen's Indian Defense** (2 c4 e6 3 Nf3 b6), the **Grünfeld Defense** (2 c4 g6 3 Nc3 d5), and the **Nimzo-Indian Defense** (2 c4 e6 3 Nc3 Bb4). It can also transpose into the Queen's Gambit Declined: 2 c4 e6 3 Nc3 d5. Before playing 1 d4 you should bone up on each of these systems.

(9) The **Dutch Defense** was once a favorite of world champions Alekhine and Botvinnik and the great theoretician Nimzovich, and more recently has been played successfully by Bent Larsen, Vladimir Kramnik, Nigel Short, and other top grandmasters. The Dutch, a sort of mirror-image Sicilian, is an aggressive defense in which Black works his own side of the street at first,

challenging White in the center only later. The main line of the popular Leningrad Variation goes 2 g3 Nf6 3 Bg2 g6 4 Nf3 Bg7 5 0-0 0-0 6 c4 (diagram), with chances for both sides, but Black's kingside has been weakened by 1 ... f5 and 3 ... g6.

Dutch Defense, Leningrad Variation

(10) This is the **English Opening**, an excellent alternative to the openings starting with 1 e4 and 1 d4. Although the English can transpose to the Queen's Gambit or the Indian defenses (via 1 ... d5 2 d4 or 1 ... Nf6 2 d4 g6), its independent lines are what make it interesting. The two main lines are 1 ... e5 2 Nc3 Nf6 3 Nf3 or 3 g3, and 1 ... c5 2 Nf3 Nf6 3 Nc3 Nc6 4 d4 cxd4 5 Nxd4 e6 (the Symmetrical Four Knights Variation). The English incorporates many other variations, some of which lead to the Sicilian Defense with colors reversed. The English usually involves a tough struggle for the center, especially the d4 and d5 squares.

19

THE MIDDLEGAME: Where the Action Is

In *The Middlegame in Chess*, Reuben Fine writes, "Unlike the opening, 'theoretical' variations are of little value; unlike the end game, precisely analyzed positions are not repeated over and over again."

What, exactly, is the middlegame? There's usually no precise line of demarcation between the opening and the middlegame, though most experts agree that the middlegame begins approximately when all the pieces (with the possible exception of the queen) have been moved off their starting squares and the kings snugly ensconced in their corner castles.

And now, you may ask, what? Without the "theoretical variations" and "precisely analyzed positions" to guide you, how do you decide what to do? There are so many possibilities! What should you be thinking about?

The middlegame is where, among other things, you try to win material, build a mating attack, or obtain a passed pawn or a pawn majority without weaknesses on one wing—that is, a potential passed pawn. The tactics described in Chapters 14, 15, and 16 will be your main weapons. You will also employ typical positional devices to improve the mobility of your pieces; exchange your badly placed pieces for your opponent's well-placed ones; gain control of critical squares, especially near the enemy king; get a rook to the seventh rank; weaken your opponent's pawn structure; and so on.

Easier said than done! Chess is not quite

as simple as Candy Land. But there are several principles you can rely on.

• First: Can you capture any unprotected enemy man? Can your opponent take anything of yours? Can he *threaten* to take anything? Is one of your pieces unprotected? If so, protect it or move it to safer ground. Direct threats must be met immediately!

But just because an enemy man looks like it's free for the taking doesn't mean you can actually take it. In this example, Black's a-pawn is attacked twice, by rook and bishop, but protected only once. What happens if White takes it?

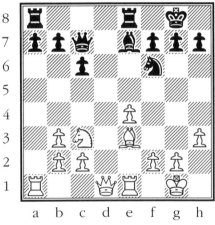

Can White win Black's a-pawn?

The a-pawn cannot be won just yet. After 1 Bxa7? b6, there's no way for White to save his bishop. Also wrong is 1 Rxa7? (instead of 1 Bxa7) because of 1 ... Rxa7 2 Bxa7 b6, and again the bishop is trapped. White can try to save it with 3 Qa1, but after 3 ... Ra8 the bishop is lost anyway (4 Bxb6?? Rxa1 5 Bxc7 Rxe1+).

After 1 Bxa7? b6

This is a common trap. Make very sure when taking a pawn in enemy territory that the capturing piece will be able to get out with its booty!

What should you play here as White?

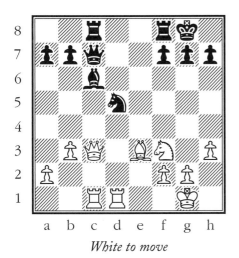

White to move

Black is threatening to take your queen, a serious threat that must be dealt with at once. Should you move the queen out of danger? Don't bother. Fortunately, you have a tactical solution: 1 Rxd5! eliminates the attacking knight and in fact wins a piece, since 1 ... Bxd5 runs into 2 Qxc7 Rxc7 2 Rxc7.

What's wrong with this picture?

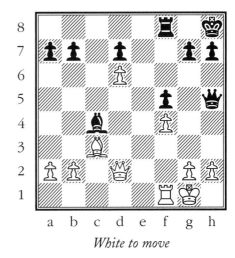

White to move

Don't leave your piece hanging! Black's lonely bishop on c4 wants to go home, so White obliges, winning a pawn with a simple two-move combination. Do you see it? The answer is 1 Bxg7+ Kxg7 (1 ... Kg8 2 Bxf8) 2 Qc3+ (or 2 Qd4+) followed by 3 Qxc4. Note that 1 Qd4, threatening both mate and the bishop, doesn't work because of 1 ... Qf7, holding everything.

• Who's ahead in material? Don't guess; count it up using the values given in Chapter 13, "Chess Family Values." Material is one of the elements of chess. The advantage of having extra material is that you can use it to win even more. On the other hand, if despite your most earnest efforts you're behind in material, bend heaven and earth to at least restore the balance. A material deficit is likely to lead to a lost game.

• Is your king safe? Can your opponent threaten checkmate? What about your opponent's king? An unprotected or exposed king is not safe!

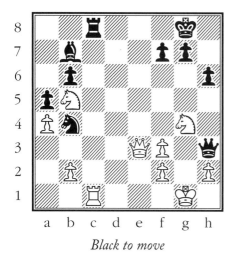

Black to move

The fatal exposure of White's king has enabled Black to get a mating attack going. The White queen is an "overloaded defender," having to defend both the rook on c1 and the pawn on f3. The move 1 ... Rxc1+ forces the reply 2 Qxc1, pulling the queen off the defense of the f-pawn, whereupon 2 ... Qxf3 threatens mate at either g2 or h1, both of which can't be prevented.

• Nothing personal, but how's your pawn structure? Look for ways to inflict pawn weaknesses on your opponent's position; that is, double or isolate his pawns.

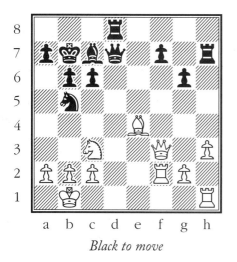

Black to move

Examining this position (you're playing Black), you see that White is threatening to win a piece with either 1 Bxc6+ Qxc6 2

Nxb5 or 1 Nxb5 immediately (the c-pawn is pinned). What should you play here? If 1 ... Nxc3+, does White have to recapture 2 bxc3 messing up his own queenside pawns?

Notice that you are attacking d1 with your queen and rook. The move 1 ... Nxc3+ removes one of its defenders immediately (the knight on c3), and White is forced to recapture 2 bxc3 because 2 Qxc3? (removing the other defender of d1) allows mate with 2 ... Qd1+! 3 Rxd1 Rxd1 mate. Always be alert to mating possibilities!

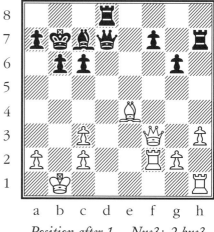

Position after 1 ... Nxc3+ 2 bxc3

In the resulting position, White has doubled isolated pawns on the c-file and another isolated pawn on a2. Doubled pawns are weak because they are immobile and must be supported by pieces. Isolated pawns are weak because they can't be defended by other pawns; if attacked, they must be defended by pieces, which pulls those pieces away from more important tasks. Doubled pawns like this in front of the king leaves the king unprotected. White will now have difficulty defending his exposed king (after, say, 2 ... f5 3 Bd3 Be5), and in the coming endgame he will have problems with his queenside pawns.

Having doubled pawns does not automatically mean you have a bad position, however. Here's an illustration from one of the main lines of the Caro-Kann Defense: 1 e4 c6 2 d4 d5 3 Nc3 dxe4 4 Nxe4 Nf6 (willing to accept doubled pawns) 4 Nxf6+, and now Black has two ways to recapture.

4 ... exf6

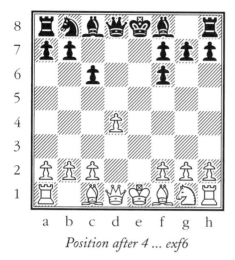

Position after 4 ... exf6

Recapturing with the e-pawn is the more solid reply, keeping the kingside pawns in a single group. It gives Black two advantages: first, he will be able to develop the rest of his pieces without much trouble; second, his c-pawn and f6-pawn defend important squares in the center. White has a theoretical edge, though, because of his queenside pawn majority, which already includes a potential passed pawn. Black's kingside pawn majority is crippled and not likely to produce a passed pawn. That's the problem with this type of pawn weakness.

On the other hand, if Black is feeling feisty:

4 ... gxf6

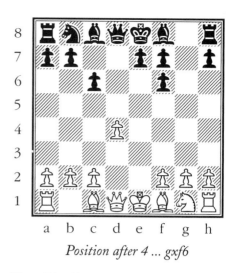

Position after 4 ... gxf6

Here Black's c- and f6-pawns ably defend central squares as above, but now Black has the half-open g-file to use for attack with his rooks (he will probably castle on the queenside). This position is not as restful for Black as the 4 ... exf6 defense, but it offers more winning chances.

A very common positional mistake is to weaken the pawns in front of your king to get rid of an annoying enemy bishop.

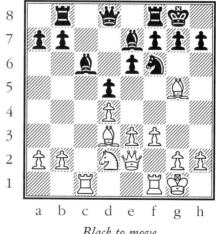

Black to move

Black wants to rid himself of the annoying bishop on g5 without trading pieces by 1 ... Nd7 2 Bxe7 Qxe7. In the resulting position, Black would have a "bad" bishop restricted by its own pawns, while White would have a "good" bishop, unrestricted by its pawns. So

Black decides to force the bishop to retreat by 1 ... h6 2 Bh4 (not 2 Bxf6? Bxf6, solving Black's positional problems) 2 ... g5? 3 Bg3.

Black's foolish pawn advances have improved White's position (both bishops are working beautifully) while damaging his own. His king's guard-dogs have run off in pursuit of a rabbit, and now he has a positionally lost game.

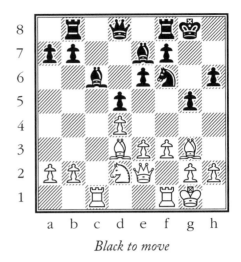

Black to move

SAY WHAT?

The language of chess, as you will have discovered by now, includes many foreign terms in addition to English ones with special meanings. Some chess words are explained in other chapters; the following list comprises terms that you're likely to encounter in clubs and at tournaments. Be prepared!

Combination This perfectly ordinary English word has a special meaning in chess. Not everyone agrees, however, on exactly what that meaning is. Essentially, a combination is a series of moves by two or more men, usually including a sacrifice and an element of surprise, that accomplishes a positional or tactical goal that would otherwise be difficult to achieve.

En passant French, and therefore impossible for English speakers to pronounce correctly. The meaning of this term ("in passing') is explained in the chapter on special pawn moves. To pronounce it, start by drinking a glass of water and shake well. Proceed as if you were about to say AHNG but leave off the G. Do the same with the final syllable. This pronunciation will serve in most situations that do not include native speakers of French.

En prise Here again, use the water and AHNG method for the first syllable. Then say PREEZ (not, god forbid, PREE). The term is a synonym for "hanging" and refers to an unguarded man that is subject to capture.

Fianchetto Italian this time, so the rules of pronunciation change. There are four syllables: FEE-AHN-KET-TOW. Remember that the CH is pronounced K and that the third syllable is accented. The word means "on the flank" and refers specifically to the development of a bishop on g2 or b2 (or g7 or b7).

Hanging: see en prise.

j'adoube Back to French, where the word for "I" (je) is not capitalized and is used in contractions as shown. The term is pronounced JA-DOOB, never "JA-DOO. The term means "I adjust." The rules of formal chess state that if you touch a man you must move it. Bu the rule allows a player to change his mind at the last minute: if you graze or lightly touch a piece and don't actually move it, you may inform you opponent that you're merely adjusting it on its square. As an honorable sportsman you should never do this, even in casual play; sometimes, however, the desire to win outweighs honorable intent.

A grandmaster got on a crowded bus, so the story goes, and bumped into another passenger. "J'adoube," he apologized, preoccupied with chess. The other man replied, "My fault, I was en prise."

Patzer A Yiddish word (from the German *patzen*, to bungle) meaning a weak player, very commonly heard in the big-city clubs and tournaments. It's pronounced POTSER.

Zugzwang German for "compulsion to move." Very often in the endgame, a player's need to make a move lands him in a worse or even losing position. See the discussion of the opposition in the chapter on the endgame. The pronunciation, so help me, is TSOOG-TSVAHNG.

20
THE ENDGAME: Last Chance

The endgame is just that: the end of the game. There are no more chances to repair your position or regain lost material. A mistake in the middlegame need not be fatal, since you may have time to correct it, but a mistake in the endgame can mean the difference between winning and losing.

Most players, unfortunately, if they study chess at all, concentrate on the openings and ignore endgame theory. But isn't it a pity to play a good game all the way to the end and then blow it because you don't know the endgame? Do your chess a favor and familiarize yourself with at least the most common endgames.

In the endgame we are no longer concerned with king safety and rapid piece deployment but with pawns. The kings, freed from the fear of being mated now that most of the pieces have been traded off, participate actively in the game, and the pawns, now risen from their relatively low station in the opening and middlegame, are the stars of the endgame.

- *All endgames are ultimately about the creation, advance, and promotion of passed pawns.*
- *Get a passed pawn and promote it!*
- *If your opponent has a passed pawn, stop it!*

CREATING A PASSED PAWN

In Chapter 9, "Special Pawn Moves," we told you about passed pawns and pawn promotion. This time we revisit the subject in a simple endgame context, with no extraneous pieces to distract us from the main point.

In the diagram below, White has a *potential* passed pawn on c5, unopposed by an enemy pawn on the same file. It's not yet a passed pawn because of Black's pawn on d7. As usual when you have a pawn majority—in this case two to one—the way to convert it into a single passed pawn is to trade down.

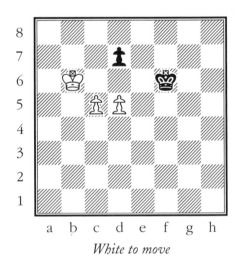

White to move

1 c6!	dxc6

With 1 ... Ke7 Black might hope for 2 cxd7?, then the game would be a draw after 2 ... Kxd7 3 Kc5 Kc7 4 c6+ Kd7 5 Kd5 Kd8 6 Kc6 Kc8 7 d7+ Kd8 8 Kd6 stalemate! The winning response to 1 ... Ke7 is 2 c7! and the pawn queens on the next move.

2 dxc6   Ke6
3 Kb7!

And the pawn queens in two more moves.

But simply advancing the potential passed is not always the right plan, especially when the enemy king is within reach of the queening square.

Here's a variant of a well-known study (see next diagram) in which the problem is to create a passed pawn and a clear path to the queening square. Think carefully: this is tricky!

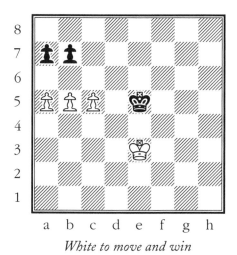

White to move and win

The good news is that White, who is a pawn ahead, can get a passed pawn with the obvious 1 c6 bxc6 but not 2 bxc6?. The bad news is that the Black king is close enough to win the silly pawn with 2 ... Kd6 3 c7 Kxc7, with a draw. Another wrong try is 1 a6? bxa6 2 bxa6 Kd5, winning the c-pawn.

1 c6   bxc6
2 b6!

White gets a passed pawn no matter what Black plays, and this time Black's king is powerless to stop it.

2 ...   axb6
3 a6!

But not 3 axb6? Kd6 and Black wins the pawn. After the text move followed by 4 a7 and a8=Q, White has a shiny new queen.

It's important to understand this maneuver. Here's the classic study mentioned above. This time White does not have the advantage of an extra pawn.

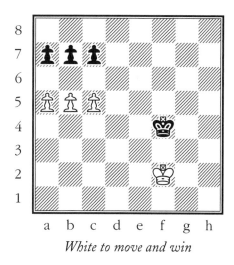

White to move and win

The same thinking applies here as in the previous position: White must create a passed pawn and clear a path for it.

1 b6!

If 1 a6 bxa6 2 bxa6 Ke5, Black wins the c-pawn. Or if 1 c6 bxc6 2 bxc6 Ke5, we get the same result.

1 ...   axb6

Or 1 ... cxb6 2 a6! bxa6 3 c6, and the Black king can't stop the c-pawn.

2 c6!   bxc6
3 a6

And White will queen the a-pawn.

PROMOTING A PASSED PAWN

White has a winning position in the next diagram. How does he wrap it up?

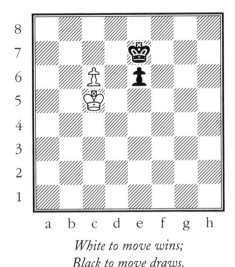

White to move wins;
Black to move draws.

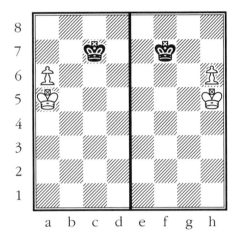

Draw with either side to move

The impetuous 1 c7? is a blunder that throws away the win. After 1 ... Kd7 2 Kb6 Kc8, White is unable to queen his pawn because he can't get control of c8. At this point all he can do is chase Black's pawn: 3 Kc6 e5 4 Kd5 Kxc7 5 Kxe5 with a dead draw.

The correct plan is to first control the queening square, c8.

1 Kb6!	Kd8
2 Kb7!	

The pawn will next advance to c7 (with check if Black leaves his king on d8) and then to c8, giving White a new queen.

With Black to play, the same idea works but this time in Black's favor: 1 ... Kd8! 2 Kb6 Kc8, and Black controls the queening square. White can't win.

EXCEPTION: THE ROOK-PAWNS

If we move the same configuration a few blocks west and remove Black's pawn, White can't win even if he moves first. With the pawn on the h-file, White has the same problem. In fact, the game is a draw no matter how far back the pawn is; once the Black king gets to the queening square, it will either be stalemated or allowed to win the pawn.

White's king can't get control of the queening square. For instance, with White to move, 1 Kb5 Kb8 2 Kb6 Ka8 and the king can never be forced out of a8 or a7. With Black to move, simply 1 ... Kb8 draws (2 Kb6 Ka8). On the other side of the board, if 1 Kg5 Kg8 2 Kg6 Kh8.

BLOCK THAT PAWN!

When your opponent has a passed pawn, capture it if you can without sacrificing anything. If you can't, blockade it; that is, put one of your pieces on the square immediately in front of it and make sure that piece can't easily be driven away. Here's a simple setting.

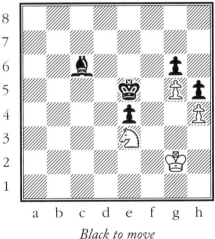

Black to move

Black's passed e-pawn would be very dangerous were it not for the blockade by White's knight. The knight cannot be dislodged, for if 1 ... Kd4 2 Kf2 and the blockade holds. But now see this:

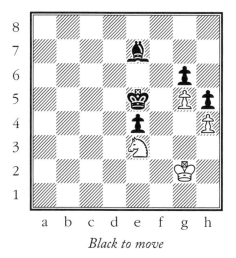

Black to move

The situation is almost identical, but this time Black has a dark-square bishop. When the blockading square is the same color as the bishop, it's difficult, if not impossible, to maintain the blockade. In this case, after 1 ... Bc5 2 Nc2 (not 2 Kf2? Kf4 and the knight is lost) 2 ... Kf4! (if immediately 2 ... e3?, then 3 Kf3 followed by Ke2 reestablishing the blockade), and White will have to sacrifice his knight to stop the Black pawn.

THE OPPOSITION

Once the queens and most other pieces have been traded off and there is no longer any danger of a mating attack, the kings may safely graze. In the effort to promote a pawn, or to prevent an enemy pawn from promoting, the two kings maneuver for control of certain key squares. A major weapon in this struggle is the opposition.

This term refers not to the opponent but to a vital strategic device that belongs exclusively to the endgame and particularly to king-and-pawn endgames.

When the two kings are separated by one square on the same file, rank, or diagonal, they are in opposition. When they are separated by three or five squares on the same file, rank, or diagonal, they are in distant opposition.

Why is this is important? Because giving up the opposition loses ground, as in the diagram below. (Ignore the fact that there's nothing on the board except the kings.) Since the two kings may not "touch" each other, White's king is prevented from advancing to the fifth rank; that is, c5, d5, or e5. If it's Black's move, however, he must retreat and relinquish control of at least one of those squares, allowing White to advance.

Here's a little puzzle: With Black to move, how can White force his way to the eighth rank? (Remember, Black is trying to prevent that.) With White to move, it can't be done. Try it!

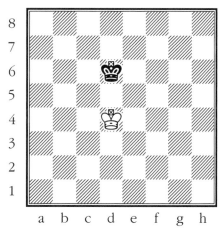

Whoever moves loses the opposition

Solution: 1 ... Kc6 (or 1 ... Kd7 2 Kd5) 2 Ke5 Kd7 3 Kf6 Ke8 4 Kg7 and next comes 5 Kg8 or 5 Kh8. Taking the opposition on the fourth move with 4 Ke6 also wins but that solution is one move longer. After 1 ... Ke6 the solution is similar.

The late grandmaster Paul Keres gives the following exercise in his book *Practical Chess Endings.* His advice for winning such endings is this: "The White king is advanced as far as possible in front of his pawn (of course without losing the latter), and only then is the pawn moved."

White to move and win.

1 Kg3!

Taking the opposition. After 1 Kf3? Kf5, *Black* has the opposition and the game is a draw.

1 ...	Kf5
2 Kf3!	Ke5
3 Kg4	Kf6
4 Kf4!	

Taking the opposition again. If 4 f3 Kg6, Black has the opposition and draws.

4 ...	Ke6
5 Kg5	Kf7
6 Kf5	Ke7
7 Kg6	Ke8
8 f4!	Ke7
9 f5	Kf8
10 Kf6!	

The opposition! If 10 f6? Kg8, Black draws.

10 ...	Ke8
11 Kg7	Ke7
12 f6+	

And the pawn queens in two moves.

THE WRONG BISHOP

Being a piece ahead in the endgame is no guarantee of winning, and most experienced players can tell you about the time they had a piece and a pawn against the solitary king yet couldn't win. What they're talking about is the famous stalemate in the corner with the wrong-color bishop; that is, it's not the color of the queening square, h1.

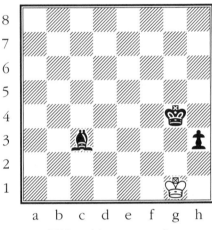

Either side to move; draw

White has no winning prospects, of course, so he's content to stay in the corner and watch Black knock himself out. If 1 ... Kg3 2 Kh1 Kf2 3 Kh2. Or if 1 ... Be5 2 Kh1 Kf3 3 Kg1 h2+ 4 Kh1 Ke2 5 Kg2 and White's king can never be forced out of h1 and g2.

ROOK ENDINGS: THE HARD PART

Keres says, referring to rook endgames: "[A]mongst leading specialists only a few have a thorough grasp of them." Since your opponents are unlikely to be endgame experts, should you worry about not knowing the ins and outs of rook endgames? Well, if you know a few things about the endgame and your opponents don't, who's likely to win more games? It's a no-brainer.

This famous endgame by Saavedra (1895)

illustrates an important maneuver unique to rook endgames.

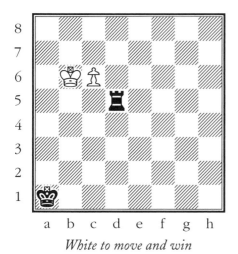

White to move and win

Even though he's a rook down, White's advanced passed pawn gives him a winning position. But if he ever allows Black's rook to get behind the pawn, the game is a draw—Black can just sacrifice his rook for the pawn and there's nothing left. For example, 1 Kb7 Rc5 2 c7 Rxc7+ 3 Kxc7, draw. This explains the following moves.

1 c7	Rd6+
2 Kb5	

If 2 Kc5 Rd1! 3 c8=Q Rc1+ and 4 ... Rxc8—the skewer in action! The ever-present possibility of the skewer ... Rc1 keeps White's king off the c-file and away from Black's rook.

2 ...	Rd5+
3 Kb4	Rd4+
4 Kb3	Rd3+
5 Kc2!	

Now the king can attack the rook because 5 ... Rc1 is not possible. The game looks hopeless for Black, but he has a surprise up his sleeve.

5 ...	Rd4!
6 c8=R!	

White sees the trap. If 6 c8=Q 7 Rc4+! 7

Qxc4 stalemate. White's underpromotion saves the win. The threat is 7 Ra8 mate, so Black has no choice.

6 ...	Ra4
7 Kb3	

Threatening both 8 Kxa4 and 8 Rc1 mate, winning in either case.

Skewer, underpromotion, stalemate, checkmate—all in seven moves!

THE LUCENA POSITION

This famous endgame, named for its discoverer, a 15th-century Spanish writer, demonstrates another maneuver that every player should know. It comes up not only in similar endgames but also in many other situations, even in the middlegame.

White to move and win

White can't promote his pawn until he gets his king out of the way. He obviously can't move it to the h-file as long as Black's rook is there, and Black's king prevents it from going to the c-file.

1 Rf4!

The first step in what has become known as "building a bridge."

1 ...   Rh1

Black has nothing useful to do so he just

waits. He could also play 1 ...Rh3.

2 Re4+	Kd7
3 Kf7	Rf1+
4 Kg6	Rg1+
5 Kf6	Rf1+

White can't promote his pawn at the moment, but if Black just bides his time with 5 ... Rg2, then after 6 Re5 White will next play Rg5 and promote the pawn.

6 Kg5!

The point, as the next move shows.

6 ...	Rg1+
7 Rg4	

Completing the "bridge" and enabling the pawn to queen without hindrance. Keep this line-blocking maneuver in mind; it will come in handy sooner or later.

These are just a few interesting and instructive positions from the fascinating world of endgames. Find a book or two to learn more. It will pay off, guaranteed.

21

REALITY CHECK

Let's see how all those rules and tools work in practice. In looking at these games, you may find it difficult at first to follow all the side variations and alternate lines of play. Not to worry. The first time you play over a game, try to see as many moves ahead as you can without moving the pieces. Then play all the moves on your chessboard and then check the diagram to get back to the game position.

The game between Paul Morphy, playing White, and Count Isouard and the Duke of Brunswick, playing Black in consultation, is one of the most famous games in the annals of chess. In 1858, Morphy, already the best player in America, visited Europe to demonstrate his superiority over the leading players in Europe, which at that time meant Germany. This he did by emphatically crushing Löwenthal, Harrwitz, and Anderssen, among other feats. Europeans were astounded by the skill exhibited by this slight, soft-spoken, modest 20-year-old. In France, the Duke and Count mentioned above, wanting to see this wunderkind up close and personal, invited him to join them in their private box at the Paris Ópera. Morphy, an opera enthusiast, jumped at the chance; besides, it would have been rude to decline such an invitation.

Reports differ on a few details of this encounter. Most say the opera that evening was Rossini's *The Barber of Seville*, but at least one source says it was Bellini's *Norma*.

Some say the game was played during the intermission between Acts I and II, which seems likely, since to play chess during the performance, as others have suggested, would have been grossly disrespectful of the singers and quite out of character for Morphy. No matter. The two blue-bloods were weak amateurs—"fish," in modern chess-club parlance—and Morphy wasted little time dispatching them so he could return his attention to the opera.

There's a good reason this game is so admired: the perfect efficiency of Morphy's attack from the first move to the brilliant finish. His moves follow one another like the frames of a movie, each move the logical consequence of the last. If a chess game can be called beautiful, this one clearly qualifies for that distinction.

Morphy   Allies
1 e4

"Best by test," Bobby Fischer used to call this move. Apart from some juvenilia, he opened every game with it throughout his career—until he met Boris Spassky in a match for the world championship in Reykjavik, Iceland, in 1972. That was the moment Fischer chose to switch to other opening moves. It was a great psychological stroke; you might call it an expected surprise. Spassky had no choice but to prepare for 1 e4 (opening preparation is a big part of grandmaster chess), since that was the only opening move Fischer had ever played. Of course Spassky suspected that Fischer might switch, but to what? Fischer won the match and the world title.

The late American grandmaster Edmar Mednis, in his book *How to Play Good Opening Moves*, called 1 e4 "perfect." The pawn occupies an important central square and controls others (d5 and f5), and its advance opens the way for the king bishop and the queen to enter the battle by moving off the first rank.

If 1 e4 has a downside, it is that the pawn on e4 is temporarily unprotected. In some opening variations Black can attack it and force White to spend time defending it.

Other "perfect" first moves are 1 d4, 1 c4, and 1 Nf3.

1 ...   **e5**

If it's good for White, it must be good for Black too, right? Yes and no. Black stakes his own claim to central squares (that's good), but this pawn, like White's, is vulnerable (that's not so good), and even more so than White's (that's bad) because White, by virtue of having the first move, will be the first to start attacking. For this reason, among others, the moves 1 ... c5 (Sicilian Defense), 1 ... e6 (French Defense), 1 ... c6 (Caro-Kann Defense), and 1 ... Nf6 (Alekhine's Defense) are often chosen instead. But don't hesitate to play 1 ... e5 if you like it. There's nothing wrong with it if followed up correctly.

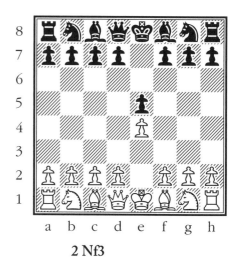

2 Nf3

A natural move, developing the knight toward the center and immediately attacking Black's unprotected e-pawn. White can start mixing it up even faster with 2 d4 or 2 f4. After 2 d4 exd4 3 Qxd4 (Center Game), White's queen may be prematurely exposed. But he can play the adventurous 3 c3 (Danish Gambit), risking a pawn or two for a very dangerous attacking position after 3 ... dxc3 4 Nxc3 or 4 Bc4 cxb2 5 Bxb2. Black can blunt the main force of the storm by giving back a pawn with 5 ... d5 and getting his pieces out as quickly as possible. Still, it's no fun to face those awesome White bishops. If such a position strikes fear in your heart, as well it might, you can decline the gambit with 3 ... d5, which will likely disconcert the player of the White pieces, who was undoubtedly expecting to have his way with you.

Also good is 2 f4 (the venerable King's Gambit), where White hopes for a lively attack owing to his quick kingside development if Black accepts the pawn with 2 ... exf4. But Black can decline the offer with 2 ... Bc5, and if 3 fxe5?? Qh4+ and Black wins (4 g3 Qxe4+ and the king rook goes). But the solid response is 2 Nf3.

2 ...   **d6**

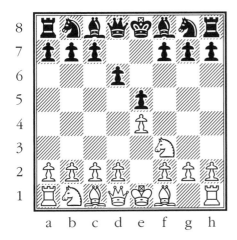 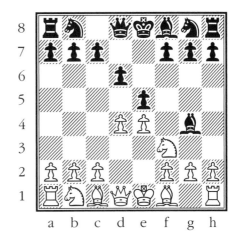

This is Philidor's Defense, a popular opening in Morphy's day. Though this method of defending the e-pawn has never been refuted outright, it does not add to Black's control of center squares and frees White from having to worry about his own e-pawn. Black has two other main choices: 2 … Nc6, which can lead to the Ruy Lopez, the Giuoco Piano, the Two Knights Defense, et al.; and 2 … Nf6 (Petroff's Defense), a counterattack on White's e-pawn that provokes an immediate crisis in the center.

3 d4

Again the most natural move. It attacks Black's e-pawn a second time, takes control of more center squares, and opens lines for his queen and queen bishop.

3 … Bg4?

Black can either defend his e-pawn and his hold on the center by 3 … Nd7 4 Bc4 c6 or 3 … Nf6 4 Nc3 Nbd7, or he can give up the center by 3 … exd4 4 Nxd4 (or 4 Qxd4), then get his kingside pieces out and castle as soon as possible.

The move played is a naïve attempt to hold on to the e-pawn by pinning the knight that is attacking it. It's a typical patzer move that Morphy must have been tickled to see.

4 dxe5

Is Morphy winning a pawn? After 4 … dxe5 5 Qxd8+ Kxd8 6 Nxe5, White would be a pawn up with a winning position (look: Black can't castle).

4 … Bxf3

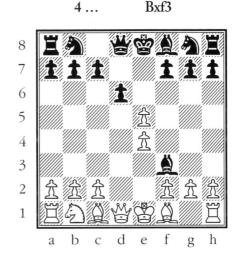

In for a penny, in for a pound. Black carries out his erroneous plan to avoid losing a pawn. In so doing, however, he loses time, having made two moves with his bishop and two moves with his d-pawn before developing his other pieces. Black thus violates a very important opening principle; i.e., not to move a developed piece a second time until the other pieces are developed.

5 Qxf3

Of course. After 5 gxf3?? dxe5 6 Qxd8+ Kxd8 Black again can't castle, but White's pawn structure on the kingside is in ruins.

5 ...   dxe5

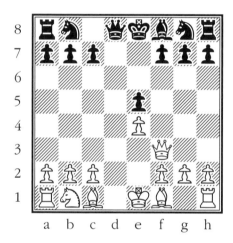

Black restores the material balance but he already has a positionally lost game. White has one piece developed and Black none, and it's White's move.

6 Bc4

Already threatening mate on f7.

The f7-square (and the f2-square in White's camp) is a sensitive spot. Notice in the opening array, before anything has moved, that the f-pawn is protected only by the king. So any threat to that square (or pawn) could draw the king into the middle of a shooting war. Look, for instance, at the infamous Fried Liver Attack in the Two Knights Defense: 1 e4 e5 2 Nf3 Nc6 3 Bc4 Nf6 4 Ng5 (attacking f7) 4 ... d5 5 exd5

Nxd5 6 Nxf7 Kxf7 7 Qf3+ Ke6 (to protect the doubly attacked knight) 8 Nc3 (attacking it a third time), with more fun to come.

6 ...   Nf6

This cuts the line between the White queen and Black's f7 and averts immediate mate. But Black is not out of the woods.

The best move is the strange-looking 6 ... Qe7. which defends the f-pawn but prevents the king bishop from developing normally. But 6 ... Qe7 contains a smidgen of hope for Black: if White plays 7 Qb3?, Black gets out of trouble with 7 ... Qb4+!, forcing the exchange of queens. When your opponent's queen is more active than yours, try to exchange queens.

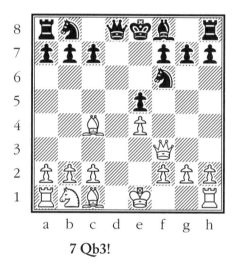

7 Qb3!

White now threatens two pawns, the one on f7, defended only once but attacked twice, and the one on b7, which is not defended at all. More significant, though, is that Black's rook on a8 would be in mortal danger once the b-pawn goes.

Morphy here violates the same rule that his noble opponents did: not to move a developed piece until all the other pieces are developed. But winning material usually overrides such rules.

7 ...   Qe7

It's a little late for this now, but it should

still hold body and soul together for a while, thanks to a tactical escape valve.

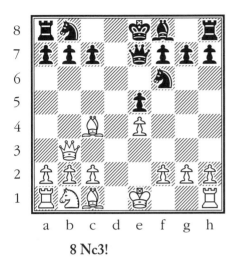

8 Nc3!

An important moment. Morphy could have gained a significant material advantage with 8 Bxf7+ Qxf7 9 Qxb7 Bc5 10 Qxa8, but after 10 … 0-0, Black has dangerous threats against White's king, particularly the square f2, while White's queen is temporarily stuck in the suburbs. The tactical point of 7 … Qe7 was to be able to play 8 … Qb4+ if White's took the b-pawn. That's the reason for 8 Bxf7+: to deprive Black's queen of that opportunity.

Instead of plunging into complications that might prolong the game, Morphy goes for rapid mobilization and a quick mate.

8 …   c6

Now the b-pawn is protected by the queen, and Black is, for the moment, safe.

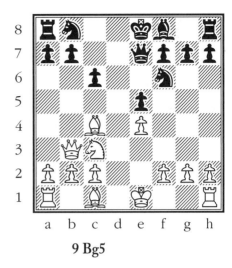

9 Bg5

Threatening 10 Bxf6 when 10 … gxf6 messes up Black's pawn position (10 … Qxf6 allows 11 Qxb7 and 12 Qxa8). Where could Black's king find safety after that?

9 …   b5?

Morphy's benighted opponents crack under the pressure. Although this move loses immediately, there's hardly anything Black can do anyway. All of White's pieces are developed and he is ready to castle on either side to bring his rooks into play.

Black might try 9 … Nbd7, sacrificing a pawn or two to get some counterplay: 10 Qxb7 Rb8 11 Qxc6 Rxb2 12 0-0-0!? Qa3 and there's still some fight left. But White is not looking for a fight and after 9 … Nbd2 can play simply 10 0-0-0 to keep up the pressure.

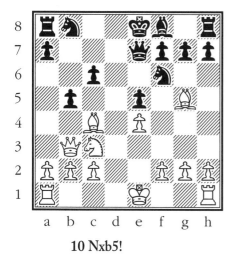

10 Nxb5!

The hammer falls. White has a big advantage in development (i.e., time) and Black can hardly move.

10 ...   cxb5

What else?

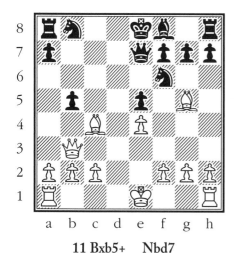

11 Bxb5+   Nbd7

Forced (10 ... Qd7?? or 10 ... Nfd7?? loses the queen). Black is all pinned up like a dressmaker's manikin.

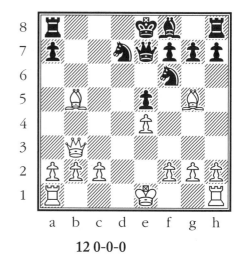

12 0-0-0

White gets his king out of the center (not that it was in any real danger there with Black's pieces unable to move) and at the same time brings his rook to bear on d7, a very sensitive spot in Black's position.

12 ...   Rd8

Black's knight needs another defender in view of the threat 13 Bxd7+, among other things. It's attacked by the bishop and rook but defended only by the queen and king (the knight on f6 is pinned).

13 Rxd7!

This is the culmination of the combination that started with 10 Nxb5. White gets rid of one of the pieces defending Black's king and adds his only undeveloped piece, his king rook, to the attack. The fact that Black is a rook ahead doesn't matter. His king bishop and king rook are merely onlookers, his knights are pinned, and his king is marooned in the center

13 ...   Rxd7

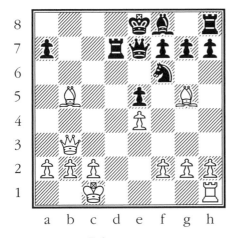

13 Rd1

Renewing the attack on d7. Black's only defense, though a hopeless one, is to free his knight by moving his queen out of the pin.

13 ...   Qe6

14 Bxd7+   Nxd7

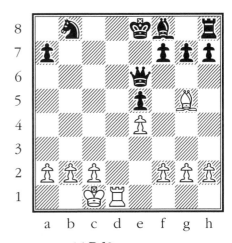

It's mate in two. Do you see it?

15 Qb8+!!

The whole game seems to have led inexorably to this crusher.

15 ...   Nxb8

16 Rd8 mate

The coup de grâce.

The losers of that game were weak amateurs, whom Morphy would be expected to beat with his eyes closed and both hands tied behind his back.

But more than a century later, it made headlines around the world (in the chess press anyway) when one of the world's greatest players got creamed in 18 moves with the White pieces against world champion Boris Spassky.

It happened in 1970, when the Soviet Union (remember?) still had a lock on world chess (Bobby Fischer's star was then in the ascendant and he would take the world title from Spassky two years later). The USSR boasted by far the most and the strongest grandmasters, and the world championship had been in Soviet hands since 1948. A team match was arranged in Belgrade, Yugoslavia, in which the USSR's ten best players would each play a four-game match against a top player from the "rest of the world." One of the most eagerly anticipated duels was the match between Spassky and Denmark's Bent Larsen, the most successful tournament player in history, with first or second prizes in dozens of strong tournaments from the 1950s through the 1980s.

The final phase of this game requires some detailed explanation. After you've played through the entire game the first time, go through it again and work out the variations. That's the only way to appreciate the beauty of Spassky's combination. Trust me: it's worth the effort.

Larsen   *Spassky*
1 b3

A Larsen "patent." Larsen was an original, adventurous player who hated draws and liked to challenge himself (and his opponents) with unconventional openings even at the risk of losing. This move has come to be known as Larsen's Opening.

The move, and the idea behind it, is one of the lesser products of the so-called hypermodern school pioneered by Reti, Nimzovich, and other grandmasters in the 1920s. One of the major ideas of hypermodernism was that that the center need not be occupied at once but can be influenced from a distance and occupied later. Larsen's move aims to take charge of the dark squares in the center and on Black's kingside by posting his bishop powerfully on b2.

1 ...   e5

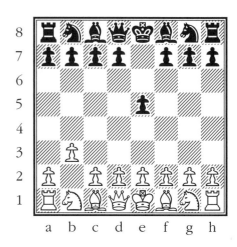

Spassky takes immediate possession of the dark squares in the center, breaking the long diagonal of White's queen bishop (when it's on b2) and intending to establish a stronghold on e5.

2 Bb2   Nc6

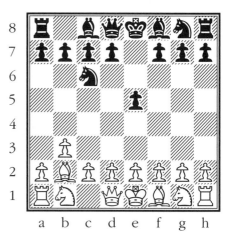

White continued as advertised, fianchettoing his queen bishop (developing it on the flank) while at the same time attacking Black's e-pawn, which Black immediately defends with a move that also develops a piece.

3 c4

White can't neglect the center forever. This move grabs control of d5.

3 ...   Nf6

Developing another piece toward the center.

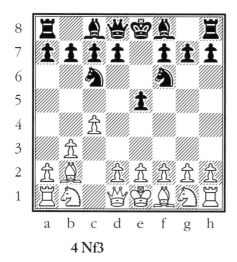

4 Nf3

Another hypermodern idea, which is seen also in Alekhine's Defense (1 e4 Nf6). White dares the Black e-pawn to advance with an attack on the knight. The move looks silly but it has a point. In the first place, White's knight is attacking the e-pawn, which is awkward to defend: 4 … d6 locks in Black's king bishop, as does 4 … Qe7, and 4 … Bd6 blocks the d-pawn and thus also the development of the queen bishop. So Black is encouraged to advance the pawn. This returns control of the long diagonal to White and gives him the use of d4 for his pieces. Of course, every silver lining has a cloud …

4 … e4

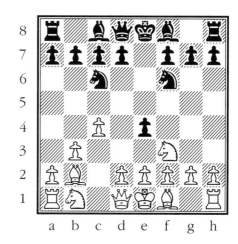

Now White must move his knight, and there's only one reasonable spot.

5 Nd4

The alternative is 5 Ne5. After 5 … Qe7 White's knight has to move yet again: 6 Nxc6 dxc6, and Black has a huge lead in development. That old rule of opening play applies: Do not move the same piece twice until you have developed all your other pieces. Unless you're a grandmaster and know what you're doing.

5 … Bc5

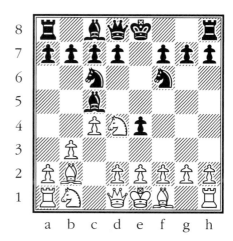

Once again, Black develops a new piece with a gain of time by attacking the knight.

6 Nxc6

He can play 6 Nf5, but after 6 … d5! 7

Nxg7+ Kf8 the knight is trapped and Black has an overwhelming position.

6 ...   dxc6!

Normally it's best to capture toward the center—6 ... bxc6—to keep a pawn majority there and allow for the possibility of a later ... d7-d5. But in this case capturing with the d-pawn frees the queen bishop as well as the queen for action in the center and on the kingside.

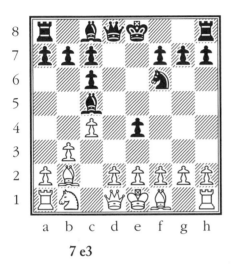

7 e3

He has to get the bishop out to be able to castle. He's also planning to free his position with d2-d4 at the appropriate time.

7 ...   Bf5

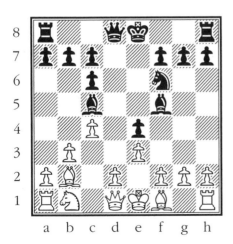

Another move, another piece developed,

this time not with a direct threat but to prevent White from freeing himself. If now, for instance, 8 d4? exd3 e.p., winning a pawn. If White tries to win back the d-pawn with 9 Bxf6 Qxf6 (9 ... gxf6 mangles Black's pawn position) 10 Bxd3 Bxd3 11 Qxd3 Qxa1, winning a rook and the game.

8 Qc2

Keeping an eye on d3, but Larsen has a little trick in mind

8 ...   Qe7

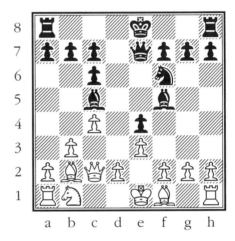

The queen stands well here. It "overprotects" the extended e-pawn, which could soon come under attack. Moving the queen off the first rank gets it out of the way so Black can castle on the queenside. It's a good idea for Black to castle there because the pressure of White's bishop on b2 against the kingside could become dangerous. Further, queenside castling brings the queen rook into play immediately on the d-file.

9 Be2

White gets ready to castle on the kingside.

9 ...   0-0-0

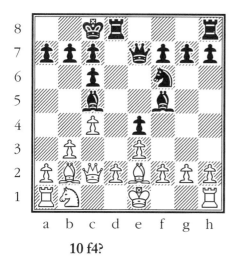

10 f4?

Thus Larsen snatches control of central dark squares, which enhances the power of his bishop on b2. Black can't play 10 ... exf3 e.p. because his bishop on f5 would be taken by the queen. This is the point of Larsen's 8th move. However, 10 f4 weakens White's kingside and this will prove to be disastrous with his king in the center and in view of the full mobilization of Black's forces.

Larsen should work on attacking Black's e-pawn with 10 Bxf6 (removing a defender) and 11 Nc3.

10 ...   Ng4!

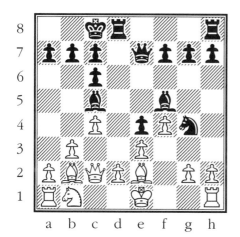

The beginning of the end for Denmark's favorite son and the beginning of one of the most beautiful combinations in modern chess. Each of Spassky's pieces is exactly where it's supposed to be, and the whole attack runs like a well-oiled machine.

White can't castle now because 11 0-0 runs into the sacrifice 11 ... Rxd2! with a variety of winning threats. So the intrusive rook must be captured. If 12 Qxd2 Bxe3+ wins White's queen and two pawns for Black's rook and bishop, a clear material gain for Black (13 Qxe3 Nxe3). Or if 12 Nxd2 Nxe3 13 Qc1 Nxf1+ 14 Kxf1 Qh4 and Black has a winning attack.

Larsen can try to avoid all this by 11 Bxg4, to get rid of one of Black's attacking pieces, but then comes the surprising shot 11 ... Qh4+! 12 g3 Qxg4 with 13 ... h5 and 14 ... h4 to follow, with a winning attack.

11 g3

Larsen desperately wants to keep Black's queen away from h4. If he tries to bring his knight into play with 11 Nc3, then here comes that nasty sacrifice again: 11 ... Rxd2! 12 Kxd2 Bxe3+ 13 Ke1 (or 13 Kd1 13 Rd8+) 13 ... Bf2+ followed by 14 ... Ne3+ and White's queen is a goner.

11 ...   h5!

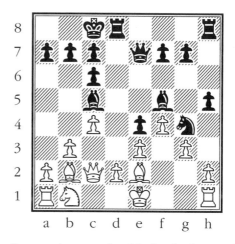

Larsen is not the kind of player who resigns when all seems lost, and certainly not when only 11 moves have been played. Larsen keeps a cool head.

Black is threatening 12 ... h4, to force open the rook-file and add the king rook to his attack. White has one teeny-weeny hope of getting out with a whole skin.

12 h3

The problem with this attack on the knight is that Black doesn't care two figs about that piece any longer—it has forced the fatal weakening of White's kingside and can be retired with honors.

12 ...   h4!!

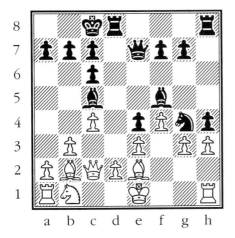

What happens next is magical.

13 hxg4

White carries out his threat to win the knight. He could play 13 Bxg4 instead, when 13 ... Bxg4 13 hxg4 hxg3 is similar to the game continuation.

13 ...   hxg3!

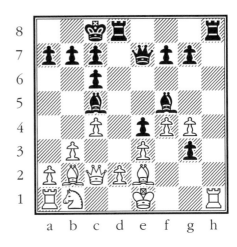

Sacrificing another piece? Pay attention now to the little pawn on g3. All efforts by both sides are focused on it. Black has already sacrificed one piece to move the pawn along and is about to throw another piece into the fire. White, most of whose pieces lie unused and helpless on the queenside, would gladly sacrifice everything he has to stop the pawn. But it's too late, too late. The die is cast.

14 Rg1

He can't play 14 Rxa8 because after 14 ... Rxa8 he'd be in even worse shape without his rook. He must stop the pawn.

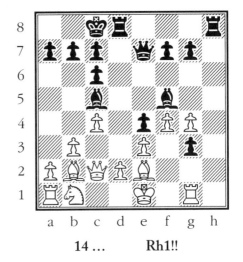

14 ...   Rh1!!

Wow! Larsen was probably holding his breath hoping for 14 ... Qh4?, when he could defend with 15 Rg2. But no such luck. Black wants White's rook on h1. Why? Just watch.

15 Rxh1

Forced, of course.

15 ...   g2!!

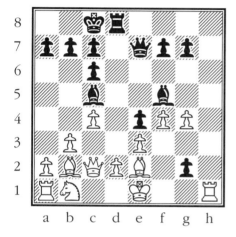

The pawn will not be stopped. The purpose of the rook sacrifice 14 ... Rh1 was to gain time so that the pawn could advance with the threat now of 16 ... gxh1=Q+ with mate to follow (next comes ... Qh4+).

16 Rf1

A heroic attempt at a last-ditch defense. Instead of giving up his rook, White could try the more reasonable-looking 16 Rg1, attacking the g-pawn and stopping it dead in its tracks. But it loses after 16 ... Qh4+ 17 Kd1 Qh1! 18 Qc3 (to create an escape square for the king) 18 ... Qxg2+ 19 Kc2 Qf2 followed by 20 ... g1=Q.

16 ...   Qh4+

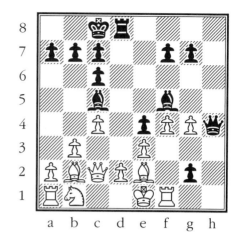

Spassky first pushes the White king away from f1 so that after 17 ... gxf1=Q+ White can't recapture with his king.

17 Kd1   gxf1=Q+

Black's pawn has had a glorious career and now lays down its life so that the enemy king can be checkmated.

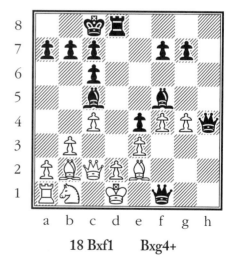

18 Bxf1   Bxg4+

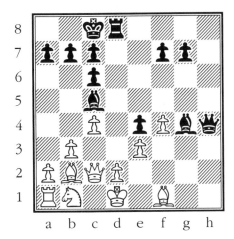

Larsen gave up, not wanting to see 19 Be2 Qh1 mate, the final move of an immortal combination.

It isn't often you see a great player like Larsen lose with the White piece in less than twenty moves. Spassky deserved all the accolades he received afterward, but Larsen was undone by his employment of an over-sophisticated opening idea that simply didn't work. The bishop on b2 combined with the pawns on e3 and f4 were supposed to give White command of the dark squares in the center and on Black's kingside. He certainly got that, but by weakening his kingside he also got something he wasn't expecting. The world champion was able to mobilize his forces swiftly and efficiently and got an attack going before Larsen could get his pieces out. In the final position, most of White's army is huddled uselessly on the queenside.

These two short games teach us fundamental lessons about the opening: Develop a new piece with each move. Unless necessary to win material or avert serious danger, avoid moving the same piece a second time until all your pieces are developed. Castle early. Grab control of the center. Kiss your opponent good-night.

SECTION II EXERCISES

EXERCISE 12

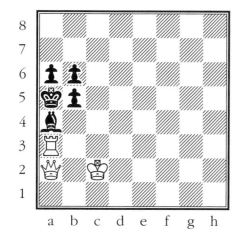

White mates in two moves.

EXERCISE 13

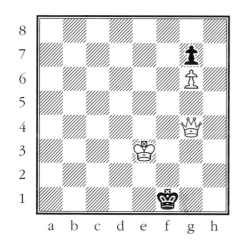

White mates in two moves.

EXERCISE 14

Black to move and win White's queen.

EXERCISE 15

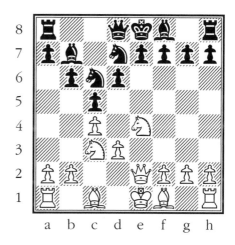

What is White's best move?

EXERCISE 16

White is a piece down and Black is threatening 1 ... Qd1 mate. If 1 Qe1, then 1 ... Ne2 wins the queen. Is there any salvation for White?

EXERCISE 17

Should White play a) c7; b) Kc7; or c) d7?

EXERCISE 18

Is White's winning move a) c7; b) Kd6; or c) Kd5?

EXERCISE 19

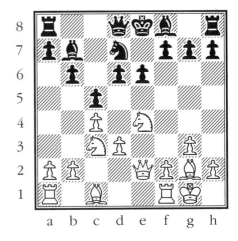

What is White's best move?

EXERCISE 20

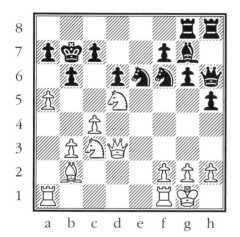

How can White win a piece?

EXERCISE 21

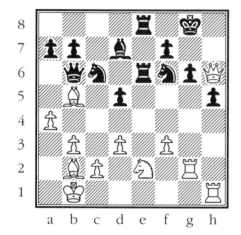

White mates in two.

EXERCISE 22

White to move and win material

EXERCISE 23

Black to move and win material

1. Every square adjacent to the White king, as well as the square it is standing on, is attacked by a Black piece. White is therefore checkmated and cannot move.

2. The Black king's only move is to take the White pawn on c4.

3. Black cannot castle on either side because he is in check by White's knight. It is illegal to castle to get out of check.

4. There are two unprotected pieces in Black's camp, the rook on d8 and the bishop on f7. With 1 Qe7, White's queen attacks both of them simultaneously. Black can't protect them both and they can't protect each other, so Black will lose one of them on the next move.

5. Black's best move is 1 … Re1+. White's king can't escape the check, so 2 Rxe1 is forced. But then Black promotes his pawn to a queen while recapturing the rook: 2 … fxe1=Q+ is checkmate.

6. The knight can move to any of its eight legal squares: e6, f5, f3, e2, c2, b3, b5, or c6. The pieces on nearby squares are not in its way.

7. Absolutely! Black can play Nd7, Nf7, Ng6, Ng4+, Nxf3, Nd3, or Nc4+.

8. By playing dxc6 e.p. The pawn is captured as if it had advanced only one square. Of course, Qxc5 is possible, but after 1 … dxc5, White is missing his queen.

9. 1 f7+ is the winning move. Black must play 1 … Kh8 (the rook on f8 can't move), and 2 Rh5+ is mate. Although other moves also win eventually, White must mate in exactly two moves, as stipulated, and 1 f7+ is the only way to do it.

10. Black's knight on f6 is pinned (see Chapter 16), which means that if it moves, White's bishop will take Black's queen. 1 Nd5 attacks that unmovable piece a second time and it will be taken on the next move. Protecting the knight with the king is useless: after 1 … Kg7 2 Bxf6+ and Black's queen is a goner.

11. The fastest way is checkmate in two moves: 1 … Kc6 2 Ka6 (forced) 2 … Ra4 mate.

12. White is in check by the Black bishop, but the bishop is pinned, a fact that White exploits with 1 Qb3!. Now Black has only one move, 1 … b4, after which 2 Qxa4+ is mate.

13. White plays the simple waiting move 1 Qg5, and Black has no choice but to hang himself with 1 … Ke1 2 Qg1 mate.

14. With 1 … Bh3 Black threatens mate on g2. White's only defense is 2 Bf1, whereupon Black takes the queen with 2 … Qxc3.

15. 1 Nxd6+ is mate.

16. The only piece that White can move is his queen. If he could somehow get rid of it, the game would be a draw by stalemate. Any queen check by White now forces Black to take the queen.

17. 1 c7 is stalemate. 1 Kc7 leads to mate in a few moves, but 1 d7 mates in two: 1 … Kb8 2 d8=Q mate.

18. The winning move is 1 Kd6, followed by Kd7, c7, and c8=Q. The move 1 c7 would be a mistake, allowing Black to get control of the queening square c8 with 1 … Kb7 and 2 … Kc8 with a draw. But 1 Kd6 Kb6 2 Kd7 followed by 3 c7 and 4 c8=Q wins.

19. White wins a pawn with 1 Nxd6+ Bxd6 2 Bxb7.

20. The knight on f6 is attacked once (by the knight on d5) and defended once (by the bishop on g7). But with Black's king exposed on the long diagonal, White is able to fork: 1 Nxf6 Bxf6 2 Qf3+ and 3 Qxf6.

21. White's pieces are swarming around Black's king: his queen, both rooks, and the bishop on b2. All that power must explode. The mate is 1 Rxh5, threatening Qh8 mate. If 1 … Nxh5 or 1 … Nh7, then 2 Qg7 mate in either case.

22. See that unprotected bishop on c5? It goes back in the box after 1 Rxe4+! fxe4 2 Qh5+ and 3 Qxc5.

23. You have to look a few moves ahead here: 1 … Nxd5! (is Black sacrificing his queen?) 2 Bxd8 Bb4+ 3 Qd2 (forced) Bxd2+ 4 Kxd2 Kxd8 and Black has won a piece.

WHERE TO FIND OPPONENTS

Chess is a two-player game, which means you need an opponent. When you run out of brothers, sisters, fathers, mothers, friends, schoolmates, et al., that will be the day you'll need the United States Chess Federation. The USCF is the nonprofit governing body of organized chess in the U.S. Membership entitles you to a national ranking if you play in sanctioned tournaments (which are held almost every weekend), a subscription to *Chess Life* magazine, and discounts on chess books, clocks, sets, and other equipment through the USCF catalogs.

If you don't want to be a USCF member and don't want to play in tournaments, you can find opponents of your own strength in a local chess club. There are chess clubs all over the place. To find one in your area, go to www.uschess.org and look around. It's a great site, full of interesting stuff for every chess enthusiast.

If you don't want a live human staring at you across the board, you have two options: play online or play with your chess computer or computer program.

There are many sites on the Internet where you can play chess. The Internet Chess Club (www.icc.org), for a modest annual fee, offers tournaments and opponents of all strengths, including grandmasters, all of whom play anonymously. You can also watch. The Free Internet Chess Club offers many of the same features but costs nothing. You can find other sites where you can learn, shop, and play for free.

Good computer chess programs are coming out all the time. Check with the web sites of your choice for the best advice. These programs let you play at your own level and at your own pace, and the best ones offer chess tutorials by such teachers as Bruce Pandolfini.

THE GREATEST

The title "world champion" did not formally exist until 1886, when Wilhelm Steinitz (1836–1900), by all accounts the strongest player in the world, claimed the title after defeating Johann Zukertort (1842–88) in a 20-game match held specifically for the world championship.

There were players before Steinitz, of course, who were generally acknowledged to be the world's best, title or no title. Outstanding among them were the Frenchman François-André Danican Philidor (1726–95) and the American Paul Morphy (1837–84). I am intentionally omitting such worthies as Stamma, Damiano, Polerio, Ruy Lopez, et al., as being beyond the scope of this book.

Philidor is known not so much for his games, few of which have been recorded, as for his influential 1749 book *L'analyse des échecs*, which for the first time set down many principles of middlegame strategy and especially the principles of correct pawn play. *Les pions sont l'aime du jeu*, he famously advised: Pawns are the heart of the game.

Unquestionably the greatest player of his time was Paul Morphy. After crushing America's best players, he went to Europe in 1858 and did the same to Harrwitz, Anderssen, and Löwenthal, the best Europe had to offer. He then returned to New Orleans and retired from chess. He was 21 years old.

After the establishment of the "official" world title in 1886, the world champions and the years they held the title were:

Wilhelm Steinitz	1886–1894
Emanuel Lasker	1894–1921
José Raúl Capablanca	1921–1927
Alexander Alekhine	1927–1935
Machgielis (Max) Euwe	1935–1937
Alexander Alekhine	1937–1946[1]
Mikhail Botvinnik	1948–1957
Vasily Smyslov	1957–1958
Mikhail Botvinnik	1958–1960
Mikhail Tal	1960–1961
Mikhail Botvinnik	1961–1963
Tigran Petrosian	1963–1969
Boris Spassky	1969–1972
Bobby Fischer	1972–1975[2]
Anatoly Karpov	1975–1985
Garry Kasparov	1985–2000

In 1995, Kasparov and the challenger for his title, Nigel Short, decided not to play under the auspices of the World Chess Federation (FIDE), and founded the Professional Chess Association. Kasparov won their match. Since then, both FIDE and the PCA have held "world championship" events, but the succession of the "official" title is in some disarray. The winners of these various events were Vladimir Kramnik, Alexander Khalifman, Viswanathan Anand, and Ruslan Ponomariov.

---

[1] Alekhine died while still champion. The championship was vacant until 1948, when a match-tournament was arranged among the world's best players to determine the new champion. This event was won by Botvinnik.

[2] In 1975 Fischer forfeited his title when he refused to defend it under match conditions imposed by FIDE. Karpov, the official challenger, thus became champion without playing Fischer.

INDEX

WHAT IS MENSA?

Mensa
The High IQ Society

Mensa is the international society for people with a high IQ. We have more than 100,000 members in over 40 countries worldwide.

The society's aims are:
- to identify and foster human intelligence for the benefit of humanity
- to encourage research in the nature, characteristics, and uses of intelligence
- to provide a stimulating intellectual and social environment for its members

Anyone with an IQ score in the top two percent of population is eligible to become a member of Mensa—are you the "one in 50" we've been looking for?

Mensa membership offers an excellent range of benefits:
- Networking and social activities nationally and around the world
- Special Interest Groups (hundreds of chances to pursue your hobbies and interests—from art to zoology!)
- Monthly International Journal, national magazines, and regional newsletters
- Local meetings—from game challenges to food and drink
- National and international weekend gatherings and conferences
- Intellectually stimulating lectures and seminars
- Access to the worldwide SIGHT network for travelers and hosts

For more information about Mensa International:

www.mensa.org
Mensa International
15 The Ivories
6–8 Northampton Street
Islington, London N1 2HY
United Kingdom

For more information about American Mensa:
www.us.mensa.org
Telephone: (800) 66-MENSA
American Mensa Ltd.
1229 Corporate Drive West
Arlington, TX 76006 USA

For more information about British Mensa (UK and Ireland):
www.mensa.org.uk
Telephone: +44 (0) 1902 772771
E-mail: enquiries@mensa.org.uk
British Mensa Ltd.
St. John's House
St. John's Square
Wolverhampton WV2 4AH
United Kingdom

ABOUT THE AUTHOR

Kimberly Butler

BURT HOCHBERG is the author of *Title Chess: The 1972 U.S. Chess Championship* (1972), *Winning With Chess Psychology* (with Pal Benko, 1991), *The 64-Square Looking Glass: The Great Game of Chess in World Literature* (1993), and *Chess Braintwisters* (1999). He was the editor-in-chief of *Chess Life* magazine for 13 years, Executive Director of the Manhattan Chess Club, Executive Editor of R.H.M. Press, and the author of the major articles on chess and electronic games for the Microsoft Encarta Encyclopedia. He received the "Outstanding Career Achievement" award by the U.S. Chess Federation and the Fred Cramer award as "Best Chess Book Editor" (both 1996). As a senior editor (now editor emeritus) at *Games* magazine, he created and edited the annual "Buyer's Guide to Games." He is currently working on an anthology of chess problems for Sterling Publishing. He lives with his wife, Carol, in New York City.